CHEF EM

EM

Empowering wellness one by one through mindful spiritual insights,

POWER

over 100 delicious, easy, health focused whole food recipes.

FUL

Plus, the chef's tips and tools to make it all happen.

Dedication

Dedicated to my beautiful husband who has always been a constant loving support system through the ebb and flow of life.

My son, Elliott, and daughter, Arabella, who are such a privilege to cook for daily and inspire me to push every day for a better planet, for climate change action, seed protection and remind me of the importance of the food we choose to purchase and eat.

My mother and father who exposed me to cooking at such a young age. This is truly where my love of food and cooking blossomed from.

My grandmother who ignited the flame of spirituality within my heart at the age of four. Her meditation room always was a place of solace and great reprieve for me.

My yoga teacher, Mary Frances, whose lasting friendship and mentoring has literally helped me become the person I am today.

My dear friends Sarah, Beth, Shan and Kiki who have always been voices of reason and have uplifted me in times of fear or self-doubt.

Lastly, to this incredible planet that is responsible for all the beauty in our world. I hope through my work, I can always bring acknowledgment and awareness to the importance of caring for our environment.

'Food and Cooking can connect us to our souls.
A form of meditation can be found here.'

—CHEF EMERY

Finding a Love for Food

I was exposed to the love of cooking at a very young age. From the time I can remember, food was always a big deal in my home growing up. My mother and father occasionally catered on the side and at one point my father even took a position as a professional chef. My father is responsible for teaching me many chef skills that I've carried with me to this day. The daily wafting aromas, the sound of a frying skillet and watching my father chop vegetables left a sensory imprint on my soul. To this day, I can still hear the sizzle and taste the crispiness of the most delicious potatoes that my dad would fry in a cast-iron skillet. They were my favorite and if I was lucky, I was allowed to eat one or two right away. I would say these are my happiest memories as a child. The family dinner was a place where we gathered, connected, shared time and enjoyment. Food and the cultivation of it through cooking imprinted on my young soul and I was forever changed by it.

Fast forward to 1998, I suffered a life-changing head injury that left me with serious neurological issues. I was left with an incredibly sensitive system that required deep self-care. Sleep, exercise and nutritious food became a crucial part of my healing regime. My parents' meals always leaned on the rich side. As a result, I took the knowledge that I learned growing up and began creating recipes that were not only delicious but also more nutritionally restorative for the body. Around this time, I also began practicing meditation. It became very clear to me that the daily act of simply sitting and being still shifted something within me. This would be the beginning of a 20-year-long lasting habit that remains to this day an essential part of my life. My injury has been one of my greatest struggles, but it has also been my greatest blessing. Through this, I developed a deep understanding that our daily modalities and habits make us and create our reality. My head injury forced me to rebuild most of my habits and as a result helped me to find a deeper, more fulfilling understanding of myself.

As I slowly began to heal, I was given an opportunity to apprentice under a well-known chef in my region from the Culinary Institute of America to improve my skills. I learned so much from him and still carry his wisdom with me today. I honed my knife skills along with a deeper understanding and sense of the nuances behind cooking. He was the first chef that exposed me to the farm-to-table movement and use of local, seasonal fresh ingredients. The restaurant grew a small garden with a variety of fresh herbs. Edible flowers cultivated there too, which we used to adorn the plates with. For me, this was my first exposure to understanding the power that nature can have on us. A simple flower on a plate instantly elevated the dish, brought a smile to people's faces, and the fact that you could also eat it was just so exciting. This exposure was incredibly beneficial to my growth as a chef and my first deeper understanding of the connection between food and nature.

At the same time that I was apprenticing, my husband and I also purchased a Bed and Breakfast which we have owned and operated now for two decades. We serve breakfast daily to an average of 22-26 people a day seasonally while managing staff and the general operations of our inn. This has provided me with a lot of experience in all facets of food, cooking and running a business. It also sparked my desire to focus more on local and organic foods. I noticed there was a huge difference in my recipes when I cooked with local and organic meats, poultry, dairy, eggs, fruits and vegetables. My body felt better and the food just tasted so much better. When food is sourced well, it does not need a lot to be absolutely delicious. This really got me excited about the power of food, our connection with it and the desire to help others to discover this for themselves.

During this time period, I also became the mother of my two beautiful children. This is when I was really forced to figure out how to juggle it all. Motherhood and running a business required a lot of full time multi-tasking and as a result, I had to get really intentional about scheduling and organization. I took my years of experience as a chef and business owner and began creating health-focused recipes that I felt families could make quickly, easily and yet would still taste absolutely delicious. This became the foundation of the work that I continue to do today and what excites me the most. It gives me great pleasure to give people the tools to make cooking a daily reality for their family and children. I think it is one of the easiest ways we can connect and make our families a priority. This will always be the foundation and center point of my work for the rest of my life.

The Inspiration

It brings me great joy to cook daily for my family and know in my heart that I'm providing them with recipes that they can then pass on to the next generation. When we teach children and families to cook, we essentially give them the tools to care for themselves in a valuable way. I think this is one of the greatest skill sets that we can give them. There is great comfort when families can sit, restore and enjoy a good meal together, connecting and listening to one another. My love affair with food began as a child being exposed to cooking, food and the beauty of the family dinner and continues to this day. It has always been my deep desire to be of service and inspire people through food and to reignite the lasting memories that are formed through this type of gathering. I hope this cookbook does just that.

'There are many times when nature has saved me. I look outside and realize the trees, the birds, the flowers are just as they are. No one is asking them to push or be anything else but just that.'
—CHEF EMERY

My mission is to help alleviate the guess work, give people some solid go-to tools, provide recipes and most importantly help liberate people by showing them that it is possible. I truly understand what it means to lead a busy life and yet find the time to cook and share real meals that actually taste good. When we make cooking a daily practice and routine, something shifts and there becomes this renewed feeling of empowerment. It is absolutely possible for all of us and I am here to help people unlock that for themselves.

My hope is that this book will not only serve as a delicious guide to get you excited about cooking and recipes that your whole family can enjoy but will also be a resource that you will go to regularly for inspiration and guidance, like a good personal journal. I encourage you to write on it, make notes and fill it with all your thoughts that empower you.

We all need a compass to find our way, helpful resources that can help one build a foundation, the hands of nature's grace, a good laugh with a true friend, the power of stillness and the healing connection of cooking. These things can bring great solace and light to dark corners. They can save you just a bit, day by day, until you can find your way. It is in these routine habits that humanity and living can be found again and again. I hope you will go and find these places when it feels like too much and cooking can be one of the most beautiful ways to do this. It is one of the easiest ways that we can instantly connect with ourselves and nature. The beauty of touching, tasting and smelling real food can rejuvenate the spirit and help us feel a part of a larger picture. I dare say it is one of the most beautiful ways we can find ourselves and bring more peace into our lives as it is an opportunity to fully nourish yourself and others.

Chef Note

All recipes that call for gluten free flour will require 1 tsp of baking powder if not included in your gluten free flour. Recipes in this book have all been tested with the use of Pamela's Gluten Free Baking & Pancake Mix Flour which includes baking powder.

'It is true that food has a transformative quality about it. When we mindfully prepare meals, our love can be felt in every morsel. Cooking can be a place of quietude for the mind, soul and body.'

—CHEF EMERY

01

—BREAKFAST

'Food can transform our relationship with ourselves.
The act of cooking can deepen the conversation we
are trying to have personally with our own hearts.'
—CHEF EMERY

GLUTEN-FREE
BLUEBERRY PANCAKES

Serves 2-4

This is a favorite breakfast in our house, especially on Saturday mornings. I love sleeping in and then whipping up a batch of these. The house just smells glorious and the sizzle of the pancakes in the pan gives everyone such a cozy feeling. I think these moments are to be cherished as they evoke emotions and lasting memories. We love these with a big dollop of cultured butter, real maple syrup and fresh berries. This recipe is also incredibly versatile as it can be adjusted through the seasons. Pumpkin pancakes, eggnog pancakes, banana pancakes, chocolate chip pancakes—the choices are endless. Pamela's Baking Mix is the brand we use in our house.

---

2 eggs
2 tbs extra virgin olive oil
1 tsp real vanilla extract
Pinch of sea salt
2 cups buttermilk, nut milk
(almond, flax, hemp),
eggnog or coconut milk
2 cups gluten-free flour
1 tsp ground
Ceylon cinnamon
1½ cups blueberries,
whole (optional)
2 tbs grass-fed cultured
butter or unrefined
coconut oil

In a medium-sized bowl, whisk the eggs, olive oil, vanilla extract, salt and milk of your choice. Once combined, add the flour and cinnamon. Fold the blueberries (or chocolate chips, sliced banana or puréed pumpkin) into the batter. Fold the batter with a fork then let rest, ideally for 10-15 minutes but it can be used right away.

Melt the butter or coconut oil in a large skillet over a medium heat. Once melted, pour the pancake batter in making pancakes to your desired size. When the pancake batter begins to bubble flip the pancake over using a spatula. Finish cooking then serve immediately.

⚡ BREAKFASTS

BUTTERMILK WAFFLES

Serves 2-4

These are a regular weekend staple in our house. My son especially loves them and the buttermilk makes them super light. These are also incredibly versatile as you can add blueberries to the batter or dark chocolate chips for special occasions. These also make fantastic ice cream sandwiches or they can be made savory by topping them with a fried egg. For those that cannot tolerate dairy, non-dairy milk can be used.

---

4 eggs
1 tsp real vanilla extract
2 tbs extra virgin olive oil
½ tsp sea salt
2 cups buttermilk
2 cups gluten-free flour
1 tsp ground
    Ceylon cinnamon
Real maple syrup
    and cultured grass-fed
    butter, to taste

Put your waffle maker on a high heat and spray with non-stick spray. In a large bowl, whisk the eggs, vanilla extract, olive oil, salt and buttermilk. Add the flour and cinnamon and mix until fully combined. If adding chocolate chips or blueberries, fold them into the batter now. Pour approx. 1 cup of batter into the waffle maker and cook until golden brown (5-8 minutes depending on your waffle maker). Serve with maple syrup, butter, fresh fruit or something savory. The options are endless!

BAKED EGGS IN HOMEMADE TOMATO SAUCE WITH FRESH HERBS AND GREEN OLIVES

Serves 2-4

Baked eggs are so delicious and incredibly versatile as you can adjust and change whatever fresh herbs and vegetables you want.

2 tbs extra virgin olive oil
½ yellow onion, peeled
   and minced
½ tsp sea salt
Freshly ground black pepper
1 garlic clove, peeled
   and minced
2 tbs fresh parsley,
   washed and chopped
2 tbs fresh basil, washed
   and chopped
1 tsp herbs de Provence
¼ cup green olives, sliced
   into halves
1 (14.5oz) can
   diced tomatoes
6 eggs

Preheat your oven to 400°F. Grease an oven-safe casserole dish with 1 tbs of the olive oil. Set aside.

Heat the remaining tbs of olive oil in a medium-sized stock pot over a medium heat. Once hot add the onion, salt and pepper. Cook approx. 5 minutes until the onion begins to brown. Add the garlic, parsley, basil and herbs de Provence. Cook for an additional 5 minutes, then add the olives and tomatoes. Cook approx. 10 minutes until all the flavors have come together.

Transfer the mixture to the casserole dish. Add the fresh herbs and olives and mix with a spatula. Crack all 6 of the eggs evenly throughout the casserole dish (do not mix them in). Bake in the oven for 10-12 minutes depending on your desired preference.

Remove and serve immediately. Before serving you may garnish each plate with more fresh herbs, salt and pepper.

MASON JAR OATMEAL WITH CINNAMON, FRESH BERRIES AND FLAX SEED

Serves 1

COCONUT CHIA YOGURT PARFAIT

Serves 1

This recipe is super delicious with minimal effort. You can adjust the fresh or dried fruit, spices and nuts or seeds to your liking making for countless options. Think cinnamon and nutmeg with sliced apples in the fall; fresh persimmon, cinnamon and walnuts in the winter; fresh raspberries, fresh mint, flax and cardamom in the summer; and mango slices and ginger with chia seeds in the spring. These are just suggestions but I think you get the idea of the versatility. A variety of different versions can be meal prepped for the week to make breakfast super quick and easy in the morning. This recipe serves 1.

This is so easy to make. It literally takes minutes to assemble and is incredibly versatile. You can add whatever fruit you personally love or that is in season. I also love this recipe because it is high in protein and low in sugar. You can make several of these in advance so that you can grab and go whenever you need them. This recipe serves 1.

1 cup unsweetened coconut yogurt	1 tsp real vanilla extract
2 tbs chia seeds	1 cup blackberries, blueberries, raspberries
1 tsp flax seeds	or strawberries, washed and whole (use whatever combination you love)

1 cup gluten-free oatmeal	1 cup water or non-dairy milk, such as
1 tsp ground Ceylon cinnamon	unsweetened almond, flax or hemp
1 tsp flax seeds	1 cup fresh berries,
Pinch of sea salt	washed and whole

Take a mason jar and add the coconut yogurt, chia seeds, flax seeds and vanilla extract. Use a spoon to fully combine, then add your favorite fruit on top. Place the lid on and let rest for at least 2 hours or overnight in the fridge.

Take a small mason jar and add the oatmeal, cinnamon, flax seeds and salt. Add the water or non-dairy milk and mix well with a spoon. Top with berries then place the lid on. Keep in your refrigerator overnight and enjoy the next morning.

EMPOWERFUL

HOMEMADE GLUTEN-FREE GRANOLA

Serves 2-4

Granola is really fun because you honestly can add whatever you're in the mood for. The dried fruit, nuts, seeds and spices can be altered regularly. The best thing about making your own granola is the fact that, once you do, you will never go back to buying it in a store again. For the oats, I love to use Qi'a Gluten-Free Oatmeal.

---

8 cups gluten-free oats
2 tsp ground
   Ceylon cinnamon
1 tsp ground cardamom
1 tsp freshly ground
   black pepper
1 tsp sea salt
2 tbs chia seeds
1 cup raw cashews, whole
1 cup raw pistachios, whole
1 cup pumpkin seeds
Zest of 1 Lemon (make
   sure to wash the lemon
   before zesting)
1 tsp fresh nutmeg, grated
½ cup unrefined coconut oil
½ cup real maple syrup
1 tsp real vanilla extract
Dried fruit, optional

Preheat your oven to 350°F.

In a large bowl, add the oats, cinnamon, cardamom, pepper, salt, chia seeds, cashews, pistachios and pumpkin seeds. Using a microplane, zest the lemon over the bowl along with the fresh nutmeg (I highly recommend using fresh nutmeg as you will notice a significant difference in flavor). Use a fork to fully combine all of the ingredients.

Heat the coconut oil in a small saucepan over a medium heat. Once melted, add the maple syrup and vanilla extract. Whisk well. Pour the mixture over the oats. Using a fork or clean hands, fully combine all of the ingredients.

Once combined, pour the granola mixture evenly into 1 or 2 medium-sized sheet pans. Place in the preheated oven for 10 minutes, then reduce the heat to 200°F and continue to bake for 1 hour. Every 15 minutes during the baking time, use a metal spatula and turn the granola over so that it cooks evenly and does not burn. Remove from the oven and let cool. Once cool, you can add the dried fruit. Toss well, then pour it into an airtight container. The granola will last at least two weeks.

GERMAN PANCAKE

Serves 2-4

This is so easy to make. Kids generally absolutely love it and it is also high in protein making it a fabulous breakfast. I personally love this on its own and my kids like it with maple syrup and/or fresh berries.

---

8 eggs
1½ cups non-dairy milk,
    such as almond or flax,
    or regular milk
1 tsp real vanilla extract
Pinch of sea salt
1½ cups gluten-free flour
1 tsp ground
    Ceylon cinnamon
4 tbs grass-fed
    cultured butter

Preheat oven to 425°F. In a medium-sized bowl, whisk the eggs, milk, vanilla extract, salt, flour and cinnamon. Set aside briefly. Melt the butter in a cast-iron pan or oven-safe pot over a medium heat on the stove top. Add the egg mixture. Quickly place the pan in the oven with the lid off and continue to cook for approx. 25 minutes until puffy and golden brown. Serve with real maple syrup and fresh berries.

CRUSTLESS QUICHE WITH CARAMELIZED ONION, FRESH NUTMEG, SPINACH AND ASIAGO CHEESE

Serves 2-4

Non-dairy milk can be used in this recipe but it will change the flavor significantly.

2 tbs extra virgin olive oil
½ yellow onion, peeled
    and minced
1½ cups fresh
    spinach, washed
6 eggs
1 cup buttermilk or
    regular milk
1 tbs fresh nutmeg, grated
½ tsp sea salt
Freshly ground black pepper
½ cup Asiago or
    Parmesan cheese

Preheat oven to 400°F. Grease a pie or quiche plate with 1 tbs of the olive oil. Set aside.

Heat the remaining tbs of olive oil in a large sauté pan over a medium heat. Add the minced onion. Cook 8-10 minutes until the onion is translucent and golden brown. Add the spinach and let cook down which will take approx. 5 minutes. Once the spinach is cooked, remove from the heat.

In a medium-sized bowl, mix the eggs, buttermilk, nutmeg, salt and pepper. Whisk with a fork vigorously until all the ingredients are combined. Pour the egg mixture into the pie dish. With a spatula or wooden spoon, add the onion and spinach mixture then sprinkle with the cheese.

Place in the oven and bake 30-35 minutes until the quiche is firm in the center and golden brown on the top.

FRESH HERB AND VEGGIE EGG FRITTATA

Serves 2-4

Frittatas are super easy to make and are so multifaceted as there are so many options. Get creative and regularly switch the herbs and veggies.

8 eggs
1 tsp sea salt
Freshly ground black pepper
2 tbs extra virgin olive oil
½ yellow onion, peeled
and minced
2 garlic cloves, peeled
and minced
2 tbs fresh basil, washed
and chopped
2 tbs fresh chives, washed
and chopped
2 tbs fresh parsley,
washed and chopped
2 cups spinach, washed
½ cup Parmesan (optional)

Place your oven on high broil.

In a large bowl, mix the eggs with the salt and pepper. Set aside briefly.

Heat the olive oil in an oven-safe, cast-iron or non-stick skillet over a medium heat. Once hot, add the onion and cook approx. 5 minutes until the onion is golden brown. Add the garlic, basil, chives, parsley and spinach. Continue to cook for approx. 2 more minutes until the spinach is wilting. Pour the whisked eggs over the vegetables and once the eggs start to get firm use a spatula around the edges and underneath to allow the uncooked egg to flow to the bottom.

Place the lid on, reduce heat to medium-low and cook for an additional 3 minutes. Remove from the heat when the egg mixture seems mostly set. Sprinkle with Parmesan cheese, if desired, and place under the broiler for 2-3 minutes. Keep a close eye on it so it does not burn. Remember to use an oven-safe mitt to remove once done. Cut into wedges and sprinkle each plate with pepper and more fresh herbs.

GLUTEN-FREE BUTTERMILK "CINNAMON ROLL" WAFFLES WITH APPLE COMPOTE AND LEMON ESSENCE ICING

Serves 2-4

Someone once wanted me to do a gluten-free cinnamon roll and my mind started churning. This is my adaptation of the "cinnamon roll" and honestly it will not disappoint. This is a great dish for a brunch or a laid-back weekend meal. It is also a lot of fun for a special occasion. This recipe is incredibly versatile as the buttermilk pancake batter is perfect on its own for a simple breakfast with maple syrup and fresh fruit. This batter can also be used to make pancakes. The apple compote is fabulous as an afternoon snack for kids or paired with roasted pork tenderloin, and the lemon icing can be used on cakes or cookies as well. The options are endless.

For the Buttermilk
Waffle Batter:
3 eggs
1 tsp real vanilla extract
1 tsp ground Ceylon cinnamon
½ cup whole plain yogurt or kefir
2 cups buttermilk
2 tbs extra virgin olive oil
1 tsp sea salt
2 cups gluten-free flour

For the Apple Compote:
2 large Honeycrisp apples, washed, cored, peeled and diced
½ tsp ground Ceylon cinnamon
¼ tsp freshly ground nutmeg
¼ cup real maple syrup
¼ cup water

For the Lemon Essence Icing:
2 tbs grass-fed cultured butter, softened
1 tsp real vanilla extract
Pinch of sea salt
Juice of 1 large lemon
1 cup confectionary sugar
3 tbs grass-fed whole milk

You will need a waffle maker for this recipe.

Blend all the ingredients in a high-speed blender such as a Vitamix or Blendtec and place on high until everything is well combined. Set the batter aside at room temperature.

If you do not have a blender, you can mix the above ingredients by hand in a large bowl. Whisk the eggs, vanilla extract, cinnamon, yogurt or kefir, buttermilk, olive oil and salt into the bowl until fully combined. Add the flour and continue mixing until there are no lumps. Set aside.

FOR THE APPLE COMPOTE:

In a medium-sized saucepan, cook the diced apples, cinnamon, nutmeg, maple syrup and water over a high heat until the liquid comes to a boil. Reduce heat immediately to low and continue stirring. Cook for 15-20 minutes until the apples are tender. Transfer to a high-speed blender. Purée until it forms the consistency of applesauce. Set aside and keep warm.

If you do not have a blender, simply mash the ingredients with a fork until fully combined.

FOR THE LEMON ESSENCE ICING:

In a medium-sized bowl, mix together the butter, vanilla extract, salt, lemon juice and sugar. Add the milk and continue to whisk with a spoon until a smooth icing forms.

Put your waffle maker on a high heat and spray with non-stick spray. Pour waffle batter in and cook until your waffle maker says it is done. Remove the waffle and pour the apple compote over the top. Finish it off with a drizzle of lemon icing.

EMPOWERFUL

EGG SCRAMBLE WITH FRESH HERBS AND TOMATOES

Serves 2-4

This is probably one of the easiest things to make. It's high in protein and I encourage you to use whatever is in season or whatever you are looking to use up in your fridge. This is especially delicious in the summer when tomatoes are in season and at their ripest. Simply double or triple the recipe to serve more guests.

3 eggs
1 tbs unrefined coconut oil, grass-fed ghee or cultured butter
1 tbs fresh parsley, washed and minced
1 tbs fresh cilantro, washed and minced
1 tbs fresh basil, washed and minced
¼ cup cherry tomatoes, washed and chopped
Pinch of sea salt
Freshly ground black pepper

Crack the eggs into a small bowl, then whisk with a fork. Set aside briefly. In a small skillet, add the coconut oil, ghee or butter and place over a medium heat. Add the parsley, cilantro, basil and tomatoes, then season with salt and pepper. Cook approx. 5 minutes until the fresh herbs begin to wilt and the tomatoes have softened. Add the whisked eggs and cook for approx. 3 minutes until the eggs begin to firm up. Use a wooden spoon to gently stir the eggs until they are fully cooked. Before serving, I recommend adding a little more pepper and fresh herbs on top. It tastes delicious and makes the plate look pretty.

02

—BEVERAGES

'Grace only speaks to us with kind loving words
so ignore the internal judging voices. Your real
heart doesn't live there.'

—CHEF EMERY

CHOCOLATE CINNAMON BANANA SMOOTHIE

Serves 1

This is my favorite go-to smoothie in the morning. The cinnamon helps regulate blood sugar and it gives me lots of energy for the day.

1 cup water
2 scoops chocolate
   protein powder

1 tsp ground
   Ceylon cinnamon
½ frozen banana

Blend all the ingredients in a high-speed blender for approx. 2 minutes until fully combined. Drink immediately.

CARDAMOM PEACH SMOOTHIE

Serves 1

This smoothie is super refreshing. The combination of the cardamom with the peaches is really lovely. Just like herbs, spices are also a fabulous way to get a variety of plants into your body while adding dimension and incredible flavor.

1½ cups water
1 tsp ground cardamom
½ cup frozen peaches

2 scoops vanilla
   protein powder
½ cup ice

Blend all the ingredients in a high-speed blender for approx. 1 minute until fully combined. Drink immediately.

BLUEBERRY SMOOTHIE WITH FRESH NUTMEG

Serves 1

The fresh nutmeg in this smoothie really makes the recipe and it can be found in most grocery stores or coops. It looks like a small nut that you simply grate. I especially love this smoothie in the summer time when wild blueberries are in season.

1½ cups water
½ cup ice
1 cup frozen blueberries
1 tsp fresh nutmeg, grated

1 cup baby kale, whole leaves
2 scoops vanilla protein powder

Blend all the ingredients in a high-speed blender for approx. 1 minute until fully combined. Drink immediately.

RASPBERRY AND FRESH MINT SMOOTHIE

Serves 1

The fresh mint paired with the sweetness of the raspberries makes this smoothie really special and super refreshing.

½ cup frozen raspberries
   (or fresh when in season)
1½ cups water
2 tbs fresh mint

2 scoops vanilla protein powder
½ cup ice

Blend all the ingredients in a high-speed blender for approx. 1 minute until fully combined. Drink immediately.

TURMERIC LATTE

Serves 1

This is honestly one of my favorite afternoon beverages. It will give you a pick-me-up without any caffeine and it feels like such a special treat because it tastes absolutely delicious. The best part is that it also happens to be fantastic for you too. This recipe is full of healthy fats and turmeric has incredible anti-inflammatory benefits. If you or someone you know enjoys exercise, this can help with sore muscles.

---

1 caffeine-free chai
    roobis tea bag
1 tbs fresh ginger, grated
1 tbs fresh turmeric, grated
2 tbs coconut cream
1 tsp ground
    Ceylon cinnamon
½ tsp fresh nutmeg, grated

Place the tea bag in your favorite cup along with the ginger and turmeric. Add boiled water and let it steep for at least 5-8 minutes. Take a strainer and place it over a new cup, pour the tea through the strainer so that it captures all of the ginger and turmeric. Blend the strained water in a high-speed blender along with the coconut cream for 3-4 minutes until it is nice and frothy like a latte. Pour into your favorite cup and top with the cinnamon and nutmeg.

GREEN COCONUT AND FRESH GINGER SMOOTHIE

Serves 1

The fresh ginger with the vanilla protein powder really makes this smoothie fantastic. The ginger gives it a very special and subtle flavor. Smoothies first thing in the morning are also a wonderful way to hydrate the body upon waking.

1½ cups water
1 package of frozen
   green coconut
½ cup of ice
1 tsp fresh ginger, peeled
   and minced

2 scoops vanilla
   protein powder
1 tsp ground Ceylon
cinnamon
2 tbs hemp seeds

Blend all the ingredients in a high-speed blender for approx. 1-2 minutes until fully combined. Drink immediately.

PEACH AND FRESH BASIL SMOOTHIE

Serves 1

The frozen peach paired with the fresh basil gives this smoothie a special something. In the summer this is so refreshing especially if you use a seasonal, ripe, organic fresh peach and fresh in-season basil.

1½ cups water
1 fresh or frozen
   peach (pitted)
2 tbs fresh basil, washed

2 scoops vanilla
   protein powder
2 tbs flax seeds
½ cup ice

Blend all the ingredients in a high-speed blender for approx. 1 minute until fully combined. Drink immediately.

CINNAMON AND DATE SMOOTHIE

Serves 1

The subtle sweetness of the date coupled with the cinnamon really makes this smoothie feel like a treat when in reality, it is a protein-packed energy booster!

1½ cups water
1 tsp ground
  Ceylon cinnamon

2 scoops chocolate
  protein powder
1 organic date (pitted)
½ cup ice

Blend all the ingredients in a high-speed blender for approx. 1 minute until fully combined. Drink immediately.

DARK CHERRY, SPINACH AND COCONUT SMOOTHIE

Serves 1

This is another one of my favorite morning smoothies. It is good to alternate your smoothie ingredients as our bodies like variety as it keeps them in balance. Fun ways to do this is simply by switching your greens (think spinach, parsley, fresh mint, baby kale) and your fruit (try using fruits that are in season).

---

1 cup water
2 scoops protein powder
  (vanilla or chocolate)

1 package frozen
  green coconut
1 cup frozen dark cherries
1 cup fresh spinach, washed

Blend all the ingredients in a high-speed blender for approx. 2 minutes until fully combined. Drink immediately.

03

—SALADS

'Stillness is were everything grows from.'
—CHEF EMERY

SPRING GREEN SALAD WITH FENNEL, ORANGES AND BASIL TOSSED IN A CITRUS VINAIGRETTE

Serves 1

This salad is so fresh and satisfying. The citrus dressing really brings it all together along with the crunch of the fresh fennel and notes of fresh basil.

For the Salad:
2 cups fresh spring
    greens, washed
2 tbs fresh basil
½ bulb fresh fennel,
    washed and chopped
1 orange, washed
    and peeled

For the Vinaigrette:
1 tbs extra virgin olive oil
1 tbs apple cider vinegar
Juice of ½ an orange
½ tsp dried oregano
½ tsp sea salt
Freshly ground black pepper

In a medium-sized salad bowl, add the spring greens, basil and fennel, then set aside. Cut the peeled orange in half where the middle of the orange is at its widest width. Place one half of the orange aside for the dressing. Cut the other half of the orange in slices so you get full orange segments. Place these slices on top of your salad.

In a small bowl, add the olive oil, apple cider vinegar, orange juice, oregano, salt and pepper. Whisk well, pour over your salad, toss and serve.

SPINACH SALAD WITH AVOCADO, DRIED CRANBERRIES AND PUMPKIN SEEDS

Serves 1

Salads are a quick way to assemble nutrient-dense food. The best part is the options are endless and this particular salad has a beautiful dimension. The crunch of the pumpkin seeds together with the sweet tang of the dried cranberries is incredibly satisfying. I really try to avoid added sugars and you can find dried cranberries that have been sweetened only by using orange juice. Just make sure to read the ingredient profile.

For the Salad:
2 cups spinach, washed
2 tbs dried cranberries
sweetened with fruit juice
2 tbs raw pumpkin seeds
½ avocado, washed,
peeled and sliced
½ orange, peeled and
sliced into segments

For the Vinaigrette:
1 tbs extra virgin olive oil
1 tbs apple cider vinegar
½ tsp sea salt
Freshly ground black pepper
½ tsp real maple syrup
2 tbs fresh lemon juice

In a small bowl, add all the vinaigrette ingredients. Whisk with a fork until fully combined. Set aside briefly so the flavors can come together.

Arrange the spinach, dried cranberries, pumpkin seeds, avocado and orange segments in a medium-sized salad bowl. Whisk the dressing one last time, pour over the salad, gently toss and serve.

MARINATED CUCUMBER SALAD

Serves 1

Marinated cucumbers are so delicious and honestly go with anything. This is a tasty light salad with beautiful fresh herbs. We always want to create opportunities for variety in our diets and adding fresh herbs is an easy way to do this.

For the Salad:
1 cucumber, washed, peeled and sliced
2 tbs red onion, peeled and sliced
3 tbs fresh cilantro, washed and chopped
2 tbs fresh dill, washed and chopped
½ red pepper, washed, cored and diced
2 cups spring greens
2 tbs feta cheese, cubed

For the Marinade:
2 tbs extra virgin olive oil
2 tbs rice wine vinegar
1 tbs real maple syrup
1 tsp dried oregano
1 tsp sea salt
Freshly ground black pepper

In a small bowl, add all the marinade ingredients. Whisk with a fork then set aside briefly.

In a medium-sized bowl add the cucumber, red onion, cilantro and dill. Pour the marinade over and let sit for at least 5-10 minutes so the flavors can come together.

Add the spring greens, feta cheese and red pepper to a salad bowl. Using a spatula, pour the marinated cucumbers over the spring greens. Toss and serve immediately.

EMPOWERFUL

AVOCADO, CILANTRO, LIME AND GARLIC DRESSING

Serves 2-4

EVERYDAY SALAD DRESSING

Serves 2-4

This dressing is honestly fantastic on everything. It is great on fish in the summer, on salads or even as a spread for sandwiches. It is quick to whip up and full of flavor.

I use this salad dressing daily and it can be used in so many different ways. It is fantastic in any type of green salad but what I really love about it is it can also be used in rice salads, lentil salads and quinoa salads, as well as a marinade for tofu, chicken, steak shrimp and fish. I will whip up a batch once a week and store it in a mason jar. It can be left at room temperature for up to 7 days.

Pinch of sea salt
Juice of 1 lime
1 tbs extra virgin olive oil
½ tsp real maple syrup
Freshly ground black pepper

½ fresh avocado,
  pit removed
3 tbs veganaise or
  avocado mayonnaise
¼ cup apple cider vinegar

½ cup extra virgin olive oil
½ cup apple cider vinegar
2 tbs real maple syrup
1 tbs dried oregano
1 tbs herbs de Provence

1 tsp sea salt
Freshly ground black pepper
1 garlic clove,
  peeled (optional)
2 tbs fresh lemon
  juice (optional)

Blend all the ingredients in a high-speed blender until the ingredients are fully combined.

This will keep fresh in an airtight container for 2-3 days.

Place all of the ingredients in a mason jar, then place the lid on tightly. Shake vigorously. This dressing will last for several days at room temperature. Use 2-3 tbs per salad.

POACHED CHICKEN SALAD WITH A MISO ALMOND DRESSING

Serves 1

This salad is so satisfying. The combination of the fresh crunchy green onions paired with sliced chicken all tossed in this flavorful dressing makes this very special.

For the Salad:
1 boneless, skinless
    chicken breast
2 cups spring greens
3 tbs fresh green onions,
    washed and diced

For the Miso Dressing:
2 tbs freshly ground
    almond butter
1 tbs white miso paste
½ tsp real maple syrup
¼ cup apple cider vinegar
1 tbs water
½ tsp sea salt
Freshly ground black pepper

TO POACH THE CHICKEN:

Take a small pot with a lid and fill with cold water. Add the chicken breast and place heat on high. Once the water starts boiling, reduce heat to medium and set your timer for 10 minutes until the chicken is fully cooked through and poached. Drain the water and place the chicken on a cutting board and slice.

FOR THE MISO DRESSING:

In a small bowl, add all the miso dressing ingredients. Whisk with a fork until fully combined. If the dressing is still very thick you can continue to add one tablespoon of water at a time until the dressing is smooth (do not exceed 3 tbs of water or the dressing will be too runny and lack flavor).

FOR THE SALAD:

Add the spring greens to a salad bowl. Sprinkle the diced green onions over the spring greens. Add half of the sliced poached chicken and save the rest for another time. Pour 2 tbs of the almond miso dressing over the salad, toss and serve. Cover and refrigerate the remaining dressing for later use (this dressing will be good for 3-5 days).

GREEN SALAD WITH SLICED TURKEY AND DILL PICKLE SAUERKRAUT

Serves 1

This salad literally takes minutes to assemble and is jam-packed with a variety of powerful herbs as well as lacto-fermented dill pickle sauerkraut which is fantastic for gut health. The sauerkraut will act as the dressing for this quick, healthy salad. This recipe can be adjusted for vegans or vegetarians by simply omitting the turkey.

---

2 cups salad greens
2 slices smoked or regular
  turkey breast, chopped
½ tomato, washed and diced
½ cucumber, washed,
  peeled and diced
2 tbs fresh parsley,
  washed and diced
2 tbs fresh cilantro,
  washed and diced
2 tbs fresh dill, washed
  and diced
2 tbs fresh basil, washed
  and diced
3 tbs lacto-fermented dill
  pickle sauerkraut
1 tbs fresh lemon juice

In a medium-sized salad bowl, add the salad greens, turkey, tomato and cucumber. Sprinkle with the parsley, cilantro, dill and basil. Add the lacto-fermented dill pickle sauerkraut and incorporate some of the juices from the sauerkraut as well. Squeeze with the fresh lemon juice, toss the salad and serve immediately.

PEAR SALAD IN A LEMON VINAIGRETTE

Serves 1

The combination of the freshly-sliced pear drizzled with this lemon dressing is especially delicious. This salad is also super quick and easy to prepare.

For the Salad:
2 cups spring greens
1 tbs raw sunflower seeds
1 tbs golden raisins or
    regular raisins
½ green pear, washed,
    cored and sliced

For the Vinaigrette:
1 tbs extra virgin olive oil
1 tbs apple cider vinegar
1 tbs fresh lemon juice
½ tsp real maple syrup
½ tsp sea salt
½ tsp dried oregano
Freshly ground black pepper

In a small bowl, add all the vinaigrette ingredients. Whisk with a fork and set aside.

In a medium-sized serving bowl, add the spring greens then sprinkle with the sunflower seeds, raisins and sliced pear. Add the vinaigrette and toss well. Serve immediately.

ROASTED CAULIFLOWER SALAD WITH PUMPKIN SEEDS AND DRIED CRANBERRIES

Serves 2-4

I absolutely love roasted cauliflower and the combination of the crunch of the pumpkin seeds with the subtle sweetness of the cranberries makes this really delightful. This is a fantastic side dish for any occasion and can also be served as a main dish over rice.

---

1 head cauliflower, washed
    and cut into pieces
2 tbs extra virgin olive oil

1 tsp sea salt
Freshly ground black pepper
½ cup raw pumpkin seeds
½ cup dried cranberries

Preheat oven to 425°F.

Add the cauliflower to a large sheet pan. Drizzle with the olive oil, salt and pepper. Bake for 30-35 minutes until golden brown. Once roasted remove from the oven. Toss the roasted cauliflower, pumpkin seeds and dried cranberries in a large bowl. Serve at room temperature.

EMPOWERFUL

LENTIL SALAD

Serves 2-4

I absolutely love lentil salads and they are fantastic all year round. A variety of seasonal veggies, dried fruit and/or nuts can be paired with this salad so use this recipe as the base and add whatever you love into it. This is fantastic to bring to a picnic as a side salad or to be served as a main entree with a big green salad. It is absolutely delicious with grilled fish, steak and chicken as well.

For the Dressing:
¼ cup extra virgin olive oil
¼ cup apple cider vinegar
2 tbs real maple syrup
1 tbs Dijon mustard
1 tsp ground turmeric
1 tsp ground
    Ceylon cinnamon
2 tsp dried cumin
Pinch of sea salt
Freshly ground black pepper
2 tbs extra virgin olive oil
½ onion, peeled and minced
2 garlic cloves, peeled
2 cups dried green or
    red lentils
2 cups low sodium chicken
    or vegetable stock
½ cup walnuts
½ cup raisins

Take a small bowl and add the olive oil, apple cider vinegar, maple syrup, Dijon mustard, turmeric, cinnamon, cumin, salt and pepper. Whisk well with a fork, then set aside so the flavors can come together.

Heat 2 tbs olive oil in a medium-sized stock pot over a medium heat. Once hot, add the onions and cook for approx. 8 minutes until translucent. Add the garlic and cook for an additional 2 minutes. Add the lentils and stir briefly, then add the stock. Turn the heat down to low, place the lid on the pot and cook for approx. 30 minutes until the lentils have absorbed the liquid and are firm but fork tender. Transfer the lentils to a large bowl. Let cool slightly then add the dressing, walnuts and raisins. Toss the salad until well combined. This is fabulous served at room temperature and gets better and better the more the flavors can come together.

"NORI ROLL" SALAD

Serves 1

This is a super fun salad that is quick to assemble but tastes like one of those fancy nori rolls.

For the Salad:
2 cups spring greens
2 tbs green onions, washed and chopped
2 sheets nori paper, torn
½ avocado, washed and sliced
4 small pieces of wild-caught smoked salmon, rolled

For the Miso Vinaigrette:
1 tbs white miso paste
2 tbs apple cider vinegar
1 tbs extra virgin olive oil
Pinch of sea salt
Freshly ground black pepper
½ tsp local raw honey
1 tbs water

In a small bowl, add all the vinaigrette ingredients. Whisk with a fork until smooth and set aside so the flavors can come together.

In a medium-sized salad bowl, add the spring greens and green onions. Sprinkle the torn nori paper over the salad, then arrange the rolled smoked salmon over the salad along with the sliced avocado. Pour 1-1½ tbs of the miso dressing over the salad and toss. Sprinkle with micro greens if you have them.

Store any extra salad dressing in an airtight container and use for another time. It will stay fresh for 3-5 days.

POACHED CHICKEN SALAD WITH CAPERS, RED ONION AND FRESH HERBS

Serves 1

The combination of the salty capers with red onion and fresh herbs in this dish is divine. Organic canned and drained chickpeas could be substituted for vegetarians.

1 boneless, skinless chicken breast or cooked chickpeas
3 tbs red onion, peeled and diced
3 tbs fresh parsley, washed and chopped
1 tbs fresh dill, washed and chopped
2 tbs capers
1 tbs fresh lemon juice
¼ cup avocado mayonnaise
Pinch of sea salt
Freshly ground black pepper
2 cups salad greens

Fill a small pot with cold water. Add the washed chicken breast, place the lid on and cook over a medium heat. Once the water starts boiling, reduce heat slightly and continue to cook for 8-10 minutes until the chicken is fully cooked. Strain the water and remove the chicken. Place the chicken on a cutting board and slice, then add to a medium-sized bowl.

Add to the bowl the red onion, parsley, dill, capers with their juice, lemon juice, avocado mayo, salt and pepper. Use a fork and fully combine all of the ingredients until the chicken salad comes together.

Take a new medium-sized salad bowl and add the salad greens. With a spatula arrange the chicken salad over the greens. You can garnish with additional lemon juice and pepper if you like.

EMPOWERFUL

MARINATED GREEK
CHICKEN SALAD

Serves 2-4

The combination of the Greek salad with the marinated grilled chicken is especially nice in the summer. It is best to marinate the chicken overnight or at least for 2-3 hours so please accommodate for that. Non-GMO organic tofu could be substituted for vegetarians.

For the Marinated Chicken:
1 boneless, skinless chicken
    breast or cubed tofu
2 tbs extra virgin olive oil
2 tbs apple cider vinegar
1 tbs real maple syrup
1 tbs dried oregano
1 tbs herbs de Provence
1 tsp sea salt
Freshly ground black pepper

For the Greek Dressing:
2 tbs extra virgin olive oil
2 tbs apple cider vinegar
1 tbs real maple syrup
1 tbs dried oregano
1 tbs herbs de Provence
1 tsp sea salt
Freshly ground black pepper

For the Salad:
3 cups salad greens
1 red tomato, washed,
    cored and diced
3 tbs fresh basil, washed
½ cup feta cheese, cubed
1 cucumber, washed,
    peeled and sliced
½ cup pitted
    Kalamata olives
½ red pepper, washed,
    cored and sliced

Place the washed chicken breasts in a glass dish. In a small bowl, add the olive oil, apple cider vinegar, maple syrup, oregano, herbs de Provence, salt and pepper. Whisk with a fork then pour over the chicken. Let marinate overnight or for at least 2 hours.

In a small bowl add all the Greek dressing ingredients. Whisk with a fork then set aside so the flavors can come together.

Once the chicken has marinated for the appropriate time, preheat your grill to high or take a large sauté pan and place it over a high heat. Once the grill or sauté pan is hot, add the chicken including some the marinade. Cook the chicken for 6-8 minutes on each side until fully cooked. Remove from the grill or stovetop and let rest for a minute.

Add the salad greens to a salad bowl. Sprinkle with the tomatoes, basil, feta cheese, cucumber, olives and red pepper. Slice the cooked chicken breast and arrange over the top of the salad. Whisk the salad dressing one last time then pour evenly over the salad. Toss well then serve immediately.

QUINOA SALAD WITH FRESH HERBS, WALNUTS AND DRIED CHERRIES

Serves 2-4

This is another favorite salad of ours and once again it is super easy to make and incredibly versatile. You can adjust the fresh herbs, nuts, dried fruit and/or veggies seasonally. For example, in the summer I love doing a Greek version of this with fresh seasonal corn, tomatoes, cucumbers, olives and basil. This makes a fantastic addition to any barbecue and can also be a main dish with other salads. We especially love this with grilled fish or marinated chicken. The options are honestly endless so get creative and use this recipe as a base to branch out from.

For the Dressing:
¼ cup extra virgin olive oil
¼ cup apple cider vinegar
3 tbs fresh lemon juice
2 tbs real maple syrup
1 tsp dried oregano
Pinch of sea salt
Freshly ground black pepper

For the Salad:
2 cups water
2 cups sprouted quinoa
1 tsp sea salt
1 tbs olive oil
Freshly ground black pepper
½ cup walnuts
½ cup dried cherries

Add all the dressing ingredients to a small bowl. Whisk well and then set aside so the flavors can come together.

The quinoa can be cooked in a rice cooker, which is quicker, or in a stock pot on the stove. If doing it on the stove top, place your water, quinoa, salt, oil and pepper in the pot. Place the lid on and cook over a medium heat. Once the water comes to a boil, reduce to low and cook, covered, for approx. 30 minutes until all the water is absorbed and the quinoa is cooked.

Once cooked, fork fluff the quinoa and then transfer to a large bowl. Let cool slightly then pour the dressing over the quinoa along with the walnuts and dried cherries. Mix until well combined. This is great at room temperature and gets better the more the flavors can come together.

TUNA SALAD WITH CAPERS AND RED ONION

Serves 2-4

Tuna salad is super easy and you can even venture off from this exact recipe. Sometimes, I really just love to add a variety of veggies into mine, such as chopped celery, carrots, red pepper and fresh herbs. Enjoy this as a sandwich or over a bed of salad greens. It can also be wrapped in nori seaweed paper or eaten with crackers.

---

2 cans wild-caught yellow fin tuna, drained
½ red onion, peeled and minced
2 stalks celery, washed, ends cut off and chopped

3 tbs drained capers
2 tbs avocado mayonnaise
2 tbs fresh lemon juice
Pinch of sea salt
Freshly ground black pepper

Add the drained tuna to a medium-sized bowl. Use a fork to flake the tuna then add the onion, celery, capers, avocado mayo, lemon juice, salt and pepper. Use your fork to fully combine the ingredients then store in an airtight container. This will stay fresh for 2-4 days in the refrigerator.

SPINACH SALAD WITH SLICED APPLES AND WALNUTS IN A DIJON VINAIGRETTE

Serves 2-4

This salad is perfect for a light lunch or served as a side dish. The combination of the sweet apple with the walnuts and the subtle zing of the Dijon is incredibly flavorful.

For the Salad:
2 cups spinach, washed
2 tbs red onion, peeled and minced
½ apple, washed, cored and sliced
1 tbs raw walnuts
2 tbs fresh parsley, washed and chopped

For the Dijon Vinaigrette:
1 tbs extra virgin olive oil
1 tbs apple cider vinegar
1 tsp fresh lemon juice
1 tsp local raw honey
1 tsp Dijon mustard
Pinch of sea salt
Freshly ground black pepper

In a small bowl add all the vinaigrette ingredients. Whisk with a fork until the ingredients fully combine then set aside.

Add the washed spinach to a medium-sized salad bowl. Sprinkle with the onion, apple slices, walnuts and parsley. Pour the vinaigrette over the salad, toss and serve.

THAI RICE NOODLE SALAD

Serves 2-4

The crunch of the peanuts and vegetables paired with the Asian-inspired dressing makes this salad so satisfying. It is a great salad to bring to a potluck or you may want to keep it all to yourself. This will keep well for several days in the refrigerator and makes fantastic leftovers. For the noodles, I like to use Lotus Foods Organic Brown Pad Thai Rice Noodles.

---

2 tbs sesame oil
4 tbs rice vinegar
2 tbs real maple syrup
2 tbs fish sauce
Juice of 1 lime
Pinch sea salt
Freshly ground black pepper
1 cup purple cabbage,
  shredded
1 cup white cabbage,
  shredded
3 carrots, washed, peeled
  and diced
1 red pepper, washed,
  cored and chopped
1 orange pepper, washed,
  cored and chopped
1 package organic non-GMO
  firm tofu, cubed
2 packages brown rice
  pad Thai noodles
2 green onions, diced
3 tbs fresh mint, washed
  and chopped
3 tbs fresh cilantro,
  washed and chopped
2 tbs fresh parsley,
  washed and chopped
¼ cup peanuts, chopped
  (almonds can be
  substituted as well)
1 lime, cut into wedges

In a small bowl, add the sesame oil, rice vinegar, maple syrup, fish sauce, lime juice, salt and pepper. Whisk well with a fork, then set aside so the flavors can come together.

In a large bowl, add the purple and white cabbage, carrots, red and orange pepper, and cubed tofu. Use your clean hands to gently combine all of the vegetables and tofu together. Then set aside briefly.

Add water and a pinch of salt to a large stock pot. Bring to a boil and then add the pad Thai noodles. Cook for approx. 5 minutes until tender. Strain the water and rinse the noodles with cool water. Add the noodles to the vegetable-tofu mixture and mix well. Add the dressing and toss through the salad.

Garnish the salad with the diced green onions, mint, cilantro, parsley and chopped peanuts. Serve at room temperature with the lime wedges.

⚡ SALADS

SMOKED PAPRIKA EGG SALAD OVER SPINACH

Serves 2-4

I've always loved deviled eggs from the time I was little. They are the perfect on-the-go snack. I created this hearty salad to mimic what I've always loved about deviled eggs and turned it into a hearty salad. The smoked paprika gives a special flavor and dimension too.

6 eggs
1 tsp sea salt
Freshly ground black pepper

½ cup avocado mayonnaise
1 tbs smoked paprika
2 cups fresh
    spinach, washed

Chop the eggs up into the bowl, then add the salt, pepper, avocado mayo and paprika. Using a fork, fully combine all the ingredients.

Arrange the spinach in a salad bowl. Add one cup of the egg mixture on top and serve. Store the rest of the egg mixture in an airtight glass container. This will stay fresh for at least 3-5 days.

"MEXICAN" SALAD

Serves 1

This salad is super refreshing and has a bit of a Mexican flair. The combination of the sweet mango with fresh herbs and beans is really lovely.

For the Salad:
2 cups green salad
2 tbs fresh green onions,
    washed and chopped
2 tbs fresh cilantro,
    washed and chopped
2 tbs red onion, diced
½ cup black beans,
    drained and washed

½ mango, washed, peeled,
    pitted and sliced

For the Vinaigrette:
1 tbs extra virgin olive oil
1 tbs apple cider vinegar
Juice of ½ fresh orange
1 tbs fresh lemon juice
½ tsp sea salt
Freshly ground black pepper

In a small bowl, add all the vinaigrette ingredients. Whisk with a fork and set aside so the flavors can come together.

Arrange the salad greens in a medium-sized salad bowl. Sprinkle with the green onions, cilantro, red onion, drained black beans and mango slices. Pour 1 tbs of the citrus vinaigrette over the salad and toss well. Store the extra dressing for another time in an airtight container. This dressing will last 3-5 days in your fridge.

VEGAN ALMOND AND WHITE MISO DRESSING

Serves 2-4

I love this recipe because it is so versatile. It can be used to dress either a vegetarian, vegan or paleo salad and is also a fabulous dipping sauce for fresh spring rolls or even for sandwich wraps. Below are three ideas and easy ways to use this dressing.

—Homemade spring rolls filled with Persian cucumber, fresh mint, green onions and local non-GMO tofu

—Spring greens with local micro greens, fresh mint, watermelon radishes, Hakurei turnips and local non-GMO tofu salad

—Local micro greens, fresh herbs, seasonal watermelon radishes, raw peanuts and local pasture-raised poached chicken salad

---

Dressing Recipe:
1 generous tbs white miso
2 generous tbs unsweetened
 ground almond butter
¼ tsp sea salt
Freshly ground black pepper
¼ cup apple cider vinegar
 or rice vinegar
1 tsp extra virgin olive oil
¼ cup water (approx.
 until dressing thins out)
1 tsp real maple syrup

In a medium bowl, add all the ingredients and whisk with a fork. This dressing can be stored in an airtight container and kept in the fridge for up to 4 days.

BURRATA OR FRESH MOZZARELLA OVER SPRING GREENS WITH FRESH MINT AND RADISHES

Serves 2-4

The creaminess of the fresh mozzarella with fresh radishes and mint is really divine. This is especially lovely when radishes are in season. Look for the radishes that come in a variety of colors. Watermelon radishes are exceptionally delicious and a must-try.

For the Salad:
2 cups spring greens
1 Burrata cheese or fresh
   mozzarella ball,
   water drained
4-5 radishes, washed
   and sliced
3 tbs fresh mint, washed

For the Vinaigrette:
1 tbs extra virgin olive oil
1 tbs apple cider vinegar
1 tbs fresh lemon juice
½ tsp dried oregano
½ tsp herbs de Provence
½ tsp local raw honey
Pinch of sea salt
Freshly ground black pepper

In a small bowl, add all the vinaigrette ingredients. Using a fork whisk until all the ingredients are fully combined. Set aside.

Add the spring greens to a medium-sized salad bowl. Arrange the fresh mozzarella or burrata in the center of the salad bowl (cut the burrata in half if just serving one). Sprinkle the salad with the radishes and mint. Whisk the dressing once more, then drizzle over the salad and serve.

EMPOWERFUL

MARINATED ASIAN CUCUMBER SALAD WITH CILANTRO

Serves 2-4

My kids will literally eat their weight in cucumbers when I make this. It is amazing in the summer when cucumbers are in season. It can be served over quinoa or as a side dish with your favorite barbecue. I especially love it as a side dish with Greek chicken wraps. We also love taking this to the beach on hot days with sandwiches.

3 tbs fresh cilantro, washed and minced
2 garlic cloves, peeled and chopped
3 large cucumbers, washed, peeled and sliced
1 tsp red pepper flakes (optional)
2 tbs sesame oil
½ cup rice vinegar
½ tsp sea salt
Freshly ground black pepper
2 tbs real maple syrup

Add the fresh cilantro, garlic and cucumber slices to a large glass container with a secure fitting lid. Sprinkle with the red pepper flakes, sesame oil, rice vinegar, salt, pepper and maple syrup. Place the lid on and shake the container well. Store in the refrigerator and let marinate for at least 2 hours. They will taste better the longer they sit in the marinade.

FRESH CANTALOUPE, BASIL
AND PROSCIUTTO SALAD

Serves 2-4

The sweetness of the fresh cantaloupe paired with the fresh basil and salty prosciutto makes this salad super satisfying and absolutely delicious. This is fantastic in the summer and early fall when cantaloupe is in its peak season.

For the Salad:
2 cups salad greens
1 fresh cantaloupe, washed
    and sliced into smaller
    slices (rinds removed)
1 large bunch basil
    leaves, washed
1lb prosciutto, sliced thinly

For the Lemon Vinaigrette:
1 tbs extra virgin olive oil
1 tbs apple cider vinegar
1 tbs fresh lemon juice
½ tsp real maple syrup
½ tsp sea salt
Freshly ground black pepper

In a small bowl, add all the vinaigrette ingredients. Whisk with a fork until well combined. Set aside.

Add the salad greens to a medium-sized salad bowl. Place a basil leaf in the center of each cantaloupe slice, and wrap each one with a prosciutto slice. Repeat until you have wrapped all the slices of cantaloupe, then arrange them over your salad.

Drizzle 2-3 tbs of the lemon vinaigrette over your salad and serve. Store any extra dressing in an airtight container. The dressing can be left out at room temperature and will stay fresh for 3-4 days.

SALADS

04

—VEGETARIAN

'Surround yourself with beautiful things that inspire you.
It can be an ignition to your own creativity. We are not
here to do this alone and these inspirations can be
a lamp that lights the way till we can see for ourselves.'
—CHEF EMERY

ASIAN-STYLE VEGETABLE FRIED RICE

Serves 2-4

This is very easy to prepare and packed with delicious, healthy vegetables. The Chinese 5 spice gives it that special touch that elevates this dish to another level.

For the Rice:
2 cups brown, basmati rice or sprouted quinoa
2 cups water

For the Veggies and Marinade:
2 tbs fresh garlic, peeled and minced
1 tbs fresh ginger, peeled and minced
2 cups red or green kale, washed, destemmed and chopped
½ red pepper, washed, deseeded and diced
1 head broccoli, washed, destemmed and chopped
1 cup frozen peas, defrosted or fresh shelled peas

½ cup gluten-free low sodium tamari
1 tbs local raw honey
1 tbs Chinese 5 spice
½ tsp sea salt
Freshly ground black pepper
1 tbs unrefined coconut oil
½ white onion, peeled and diced

Rinse the rice under cold water. If using a rice cooker add the rice together with water and a pinch of salt and set the timer accordingly (make sure to adjust the time appropriately if using brown rice). If you do not have a rice cooker, add the rinsed rice to a medium-sized pot and then add water. Place the lid on and cook over a high heat until the water comes to a boil. Reduce heat to low and continue cooking with the lid on. Cook approx. 30 minutes and do not uncover the pot to check the rice while cooking (30 minutes for white rice and 45 minutes for brown rice). Remove from the heat and let the rice rest for 10 minutes then fork fluff and set aside.

Wash and prep all of your ginger, garlic, onion, kale, red pepper and broccoli. Place your frozen peas in a small bowl so they can thaw (do not worry if they are not completely thawed by the time you're ready to cook—add them anyway) or use freshly-shelled peas.

In a small bowl, add the tamari, honey, Chinese 5 spice, salt and pepper. Whisk with a fork then set aside.

In a very large skillet or wok, heat the coconut oil over a high heat. Add the onion and sauté 5-6 minutes until the onion begins to brown. Add the garlic and ginger and continue to stir. Reduce heat to medium and add the kale, red pepper and broccoli. Continue to cook, stirring frequently so the veggies do not burn. Cook 8-10 minutes until the veggies are tender. Add the rice and peas and continue to stir quickly for 1 more minute.

Add the tamari and honey mixture and reduce heat to low. Use your wooden spoon to fully combine and evenly distribute the sauce through the veggies and rice. Serve immediately.

GARLIC MASHED POTATOES

Serves 2-4

This is a regular staple in our home and my father who was a chef himself taught me a brilliant chef trick that takes these mashed potatoes to another level. Everyone in our house absolutely loves these and they can be paired with so many dishes. Fish, pork tenderloin, steaks or as the topping for Shepard's pie.

Pinch of sea salt
6-8 potatoes, washed, peeled and cut
3 garlic cloves, peeled

2 tbs cultured butter
¾ cup buttermilk
1 tsp sea salt
Freshly ground black pepper

Fill a large stock pot with cold water and a pinch of salt, then add the potatoes and garlic. Place the pot on the stovetop over a high heat. Once the water comes to a boil reduce heat to medium-low and cook approx. 25 minutes until the potatoes are fork tender. Drain the water from the pot making sure to leave the softened garlic. Add the butter and let it melt, then add the buttermilk, salt and pepper. Use a fork or an electric beater to mash well until the potatoes are nice and smooth. Additional salt or pepper can be added to your liking.

BORSCHT

Serves 2-4

This quick, vegetarian/vegan recipe is especially delicious when beets and corn are in season. This particular soup even tastes better on the second day so if you're having guests, it could be made the night before. I love topping it with a touch of cultured sour cream or vegan plain coconut yogurt and then finishing it off with some fresh dill.

2 tbs extra virgin olive oil
3 garlic cloves, peeled and minced
2 tbs herbs de Provence
4 beets, washed, peeled and cubed
2 small potatoes, washed, peeled and cubed

2 ears of fresh corn, peeled and the corn taken off the cob (omit if not corn season)
2 cups stock or low sodium vegetable stock
¼ cup apple cider vinegar
1 tsp sea salt
Freshly ground black pepper
1 tbs real maple syrup

Heat the olive oil in a large stock pot over a medium heat. Add the garlic and herbs de Provence and sauté for 2 minutes, stirring continuously so the garlic does not burn. Add the beets, potatoes and corn. Then add the vegetable stock, apple cider vinegar, salt, pepper and maple syrup. Increase the heat and bring to a quick boil, then reduce to low and cook 25-30 minutes until the potatoes and beets are tender.

VEGETARIAN

SPRING ROLLS WITH ALMOND CHILI SAUCE

Serves 2-4

I absolutely love fresh spring rolls and you can put just about whatever you want in them. You can make them super simple or fancy them up. They are especially good if you add sautéed shallots and bean thread noodles but I tried to keep this recipe fairly simple so that it wouldn't be too labor intensive. These are especially fun for a party!

For the Almond Chili Sauce:
½ cup almond butter
¼ cup water
¼ tsp red chili pepper flakes
2 tbs rice vinegar
1 tbs raw local honey
Pinch of sea salt
Freshly ground black pepper

8-10 rice papers
1 red pepper, washed, cored and cut into matchsticks
1 carrot, washed, peeled and cut into matchsticks
1 cucumber, washed, peeled and cut into matchsticks
1 avocado, washed, pit removed and sliced thinly
1 bunch of fresh basil, washed

In a small bowl add the almond butter, water, red chili, rice vinegar, honey, salt and pepper. Whisk well then set aside so the flavors can come together.

Wash and cut all the vegetables into matchsticks and place on a large plate so assembly can be easy. Add fairly hot water to a large pan. Place one rice paper into the hot water, and remove once just softened. Place on a plate and add a little red pepper, carrot, cucumber, avocado and fresh basil. Fold the rice paper up on each end around the vegetables, then roll it up (like you would a burrito). Place on a clean dry plate and then continue assembling until all of your rice papers have been used up. Place a wet cloth over the finished spring rolls so they do not dry out. Once you have assembled them all, arrange them on a plate with the almond dipping sauce.

EMPOWERFUL

⚡   VEGETARIAN

VEGGIE BURGERS

Serves 2-4

When I created this recipe, in particular, it stirred from wanting a really delicious veggie burger that didn't crumble or taste like sawdust. I hate to say it but many veggie burgers just fall short in terms of flavor and consistency. This, however, is not your typical veggie burger and this recipe is a huge success in our house. My kids absolutely love these and they are a lot of fun too as they can be dressed up in so many ways. Think pickles, sauerkraut, roasted poblanos, cheese, red onion, lettuce, micro greens, sautéed onions and mushrooms. The options are endless. I also love that I can get two meals out of this recipe which is fantastic on busy days when you just need to get dinner on the table fast. Chef's note ** You will need a food processor for this recipe.

---

2 tbs extra virgin olive oil
½ onion, peeled and minced
1 tsp sea salt
Freshly ground black pepper
2 garlic cloves, peeled
    and minced
1 tbs ground cumin
1 tbs ground chili
1 cup raw walnuts
2 cans pinto beans or
    kidney beans, washed
    and drained
2 eggs
1 cup gluten-free
    breadcrumbs or regular
    breadcrumbs (please
    have extra set aside
    to reach proper
    consistency)

Heat 1 tbp of the olive oil in a large skillet over a medium heat. Add the onion, salt and pepper and cook for 7-8 minutes until golden brown. Add the garlic, cumin, chili and walnuts. Continue to cook for an additional 5 minutes. Once cooked, set aside briefly.

Add the beans, eggs and the walnut/onion mixture to a food processor. Purée on high until combined, then add the breadcrumbs and continue to pulse until the ingredients are fully mixed. Using a spatula, transfer the bean mixture from the food processor to a large bowl. Add approx. ½ cup additional bread crumbs until the mixture is not super sticky and you can form it into individual burgers using your hands. This recipe will yield a total of 8 burgers. I double wrap the additional 4 burgers in eco-friendly plastic wrap and place them in the freezer for another day.

Once you're ready to cook the burgers, heat the remaining oil in a large skillet over a medium heat. Brown the burger on one side then flip it over (approx. 4 minutes per side). Serve on buns or over a salad with your favorite fixings.

CAULIFLOWER PIZZA CRUST

Serves 2-4

Cauliflower pizza crust is surprisingly tasty and the options are endless just like with a regular pizza. This is a really fun Sunday project. I love mine with sliced peppers, spinach, fresh garlic, basil and cheese. Top yours with whatever you like.

---

2 tbs extra virgin olive oil
½ onion, peeled and minced
2 garlic cloves, minced
1 tsp dried oregano
Pinch of sea salt
Freshly ground black pepper
1 head cauliflower, washed, cored, chopped, then riced in a food processor
½ cup Parmesan Reggiano
2 eggs, beaten

Preheat oven to 375°F.

Heat the olive oil in a large skillet over a medium heat. Add the minced onions and garlic and cook for approx. 8 minutes until the onion is translucent. Season with the oregano, salt and pepper. Add the riced cauliflower and continue to cook until the cauliflower is tender, approx. 8 minutes. Once cooked, remove from heat and briefly set aside.

Transfer the sautéed cauliflower mixture to a medium-sized bowl. Let the mixture cool for a few minutes. Add the cheese and beaten eggs. Mix until fully combined and set aside briefly.

Coat a pizza stone or cookie sheet with a little olive oil or parchment paper. Press the cauliflower mixture into whatever shape you like making it evenly ¼-½ inch thick. Bake in the oven until golden brown for 10 minutes. Remove from oven and add your favorite toppings. Once topped put the crust back in the oven, bake for an additional 10 minutes until golden brown and serve.

COWBOY CAVIAR

Serves 2-4

This is honestly one of my favorite dishes. It is easy to make and is fantastic with tortilla chips, over salad greens or with tuna fish. It also makes great meal prep for the week as it can be stored in an airtight container in the fridge for at least 5-6 days. I love bringing this to potlucks!

1 can black beans,
  drained and washed
1 can black eyed peas,
  drained and washed
3 stalks celery, washed,
  ribs removed and diced
½ red onion, washed,
  peeled and minced
2 avocados, washed,
  pits removed and diced
1½ red peppers, washed,
  cored and diced
1 green pepper, washed,
  cored and diced
2 tomatoes, washed,
  cored and diced
3 tbs green onion,
  washed and diced
3 tbs fresh cilantro,
  washed and minced
1 Jalapeño, washed,
  deseeded and
  diced (optional)

For the Dressing:
½ cup extra virgin olive oil
½ cup apple cider vinegar
2 tbs real maple syrup
1 tsp dried oregano
1 tsp sea salt
Freshly ground black pepper
Juice of 1 lime

In a large bowl, add the black beans, black eyed peas, celery, red onion, avocados, red pepper, green pepper, tomatoes, green onion, cilantro and jalapeño. Toss until all the ingredients are well combined, then set aside briefly.

Add all the dressing ingredients to a small bowl. Whisk well with a fork, then pour over the caviar. Toss the caviar well, then let marinate at room temperature for at least 30 minutes. This will get better the longer the flavors can come together.

ZUCCHINI WITH FRESH MINT AND PEAS

This is such a simple, easy recipe to prepare and literally takes minutes. It is especially delicious in the summer when everyone is trying to figure out what to do with all that fresh, seasonal zucchini. My other favorite part about summer is the fresh sweet pea season. We eat them like snacks just popping them out of the shells as they are so sweet and absolutely delicious. The fresh mint paired with the sweet peas and salty Parmesan really elevates this dish. I generally put my zucchini through my food processor to get that ribbon like slice but you can use a knife and just chop them thinly too as an alternative.

4 zucchinis, washed, cut
    into ribbons
¼ cup fresh mint, washed
    and torn
1 cup fresh peas, shelled
½ cup Parmesan
    Reggiano, shredded
1 tsp sea salt
Freshly ground black pepper
1 tbs fresh lemon juice
3 tbs extra virgin olive oil

Arrange the zucchini in a large bowl and add the mint, shelled peas, Parmesan, salt and pepper. Drizzle the salad with the fresh lemon juice and olive oil. Toss lightly so the ingredients can fully combine. This salad is great right away and gets even better if you can let it rest for 30 minutes so all the flavors can come together.

GAZPACHO

Serves 2-4

Gazpacho plausibly might be one of my favorite things especially in the summer when tomatoes, peppers and cucumbers are in their peak season. It is so refreshing on a hot day and I love that this will store in your refrigerator for at least 6-7 days in an airtight container. This is a fantastic recipe to make as meal prep on the weekend for delicious meals on-the-go all week. I love the versatility of gazpacho too as it is delicious just as is or it can be topped with fresh herbs, green onions, hot sauce, a dollop of sour cream or vegan plain coconut yogurt and sliced avocados. Honestly, the options are endless.

Juice of ½ lime
Juice of 1 lemon
¼ cup extra virgin olive oil
½ cup white vinegar
2 tbs Worcestershire sauce
2 cups bottled
    vegetable juice

4 large tomatoes, washed,
    cored and chopped
1 garlic clove, peeled
2 cucumbers, washed,
    peeled and chopped
2 red peppers, washed,
    cored and chopped
1 tbs fresh cilantro, washed
1 tbs fresh parsley, washed
1 tbs fresh dill
1 tsp sea salt
Freshly ground black pepper

In a medium-sized bowl, add the lime juice, lemon juice, oil, vinegar, Worcestershire sauce and vegetable juice. Whisk well then set aside briefly so the flavors can come together.

Use a food processor or manually chop all of the vegetables and fresh herbs, then transfer to a large bowl. Pour the vegetable juice mixture over the finely chopped vegetables and toss well. Season with salt and pepper. Ideally, let this sit at room temperature for 1-2 hours or overnight in the refrigerator so the flavors can come together. This soup will taste better the more time it has to rest.

⚡   VEGETARIAN

WALNUT PÂTÉ

Serves 2-4

Vegan pâtés like this one are so simple to make and taste incredible. It is really fun to serve this on a big cheese board with lots of crackers, dried fruit, olives, sliced veggies and local honey.

1½ cups raw walnuts (soaked for at least 2 hours in water)
1 tbs extra virgin olive oil
2 small shallots, peeled and diced
1 garlic clove, peeled and minced
2 tbs green onions, washed and diced
Pinch of sea salt
Freshly ground black pepper
2 tbs gluten-free low sodium tamari
¼ cup water

Fill a medium-sized bowl with cool water, add the walnuts and soak for at least 2 hours.

Heat the olive oil in a large sauté pan over a medium heat. Add the shallots, garlic, green onions, salt and pepper. Sauté for approx. 8 minutes until the shallots are golden brown. Set aside.

Drain the soaked walnuts, then transfer them to your food processor. Add the shallots and fresh herb mixture, together with the tamari and pulse the mixture until it combines. Add the water slowly until the mixture becomes smooth (up to ¼ cup). Store in an airtight container. This will last for up to 7 days.

CASHEW CHEESE

Serves 2-4

Vegan cheese can actually be incredibly satisfying. It is fantastic drizzled over roasted veggie bowls or on steamed broccoli and makes a fabulous spread for sandwiches.

1½ cups raw cashews (soaked for at least 2 hours in water)
1 tbs extra virgin olive oil
2 small shallots, peeled and diced
1 garlic cloves, peeled and minced
2 tbs green onions, washed and diced
1 tsp sea salt
Freshly ground black pepper
Juice of 1 lemon
2 tbs nutritional yeast
¼ cup water

Fill a medium-sized bowl with cool water, add the cashews and soak for at least 2 hours.

Add olive oil to a large sauté pan over a medium heat. Add the shallots, garlic, green onions, salt and pepper. Sauté approx. 8 minutes until the shallots are golden brown. Set aside.

Drain the soaked cashews, then transfer them to your food processor. Add the shallots and fresh herb mixture. Add the lemon juice and yeast, then begin to pulse the mixture until it begins to combine. Add the water slowly until the mixture becomes smooth (up to ¼ cup).

Store in an airtight container. This will last for up to 7 days.

⚡   VEGETARIAN

CABBAGE ROLLS STUFFED WITH SPROUTED LENTILS AND VEGGIES

Serves 2-4

This is a really lovely vegetarian recipe that is hardy and satisfying. We especially love this in the cooler months in fall or winter as it is so comforting. Using sprouted grains whenever possible is a wonderful way to add more nutrient-dense foods to your diet. These sprouted foods are actually live grains and as a result the nutrients are more bioavailable to the body. For the artichoke tomato sauce, I love Rao's Homemade brand.

---

1 green cabbage, washed, cabbage leaves peeled off
1 tbs extra virgin olive oil
1 tbs herbs de Provence
1 tbs dried oregano
1 medium yellow onion, peeled and minced
4 garlic cloves, peeled and minced
2 stalks celery, washed and chopped
2 carrots, washed, peeled and chopped
1 tsp yellow curry powder
4 cups of a mix of sprouted green lentils, adzuki and quinoa (true roots make a great medley)
2 jars (24oz) artichoke tomato sauce (refill one of the tomato jars with water and add to a casserole dish)
Pinch of sea salt
Freshly ground black pepper
2 cups water

Preheat oven to 400°F degrees.

Fill a large stock pot with water, add a pinch of sea salt and place over a high heat. Once boiling add the cabbage leaves and blanch for 5 minutes. Remove from heat, drain the water and immediately transfer the leaves to a bowl of cool water then set them aside.

Heat the olive oil in the now-empty stock pot over a medium heat. Add the herbs de Provence, oregano and onion and cook approx. 8 minutes until the onions are translucent. Add the garlic, celery, carrots and curry powder and cook for another 5 minutes until the veggies become tender. Add the sprouted lentils, tomato sauce, salt, pepper and water. Bring to a boil by placing heat on high, then reduce heat to low and let the mixture cook down for 15-20 minutes until the lentils are just tender. Remove from heat and let cool briefly.

In a casserole dish, arrange the cabbage leaves. Add the lentil mixture to each individual cabbage leaf and fold the leaves over. Keep repeating this until all your cabbage leaves and the lentil mixture are gone.

Bake in the oven for one hour. Serve hot.

CURRIED LENTIL DAHL

Serves 2-4

This recipe is on a regular rotation in our home because it is very quick, super healthy and, most importantly, it tastes divine. My kids really love it and its fun because each person can individually customize their bowl. I personally like mine with a dollop of coconut yogurt, fresh cilantro, sweet raisins and mango chutney. It can really be fancied up in a way that is great for entertaining too, especially if you're accommodating someone who follows a vegan diet.

---

1 tbs unrefined coconut oil
1 medium onion, peeled
   and diced
Pinch of sea salt
Freshly ground black pepper
1 tbs fresh ginger, washed,
   peeled and minced
2 garlic cloves, peeled
   and minced
¼ cup fresh cilantro,
   washed and minced
2 tbs mild curry powder
   (spicy curry powder
   may be used if that is
   your preference)
1½ cups red lentils
1 medium head of
   cauliflower, washed
   and cut into
   bite-size pieces
32floz. low-sodium
   vegetable stock or
   homemade stock
2 tbs sweet mango
   chutney (optional)
¼ cup raisins

Heat the coconut oil in a medium-sized stock pot with a lid over a medium heat. Add the onion, salt and pepper. Sauté for approx. 8 minutes until the onions are translucent, then add the minced ginger, garlic, cilantro and 1 tbs of the curry powder. Cook 2-3 minutes then add the red lentils and cauliflower. Stir quickly then immediately add the stock as well as the remaining curry powder and the mango chutney. Bring the heat up to high until the curry just begins to simmer then immediately reduce to low. Add the raisins then place the top on the pot and let cook for 10-15 minutes. The liquid will reduce.

I generally serve this with steamed basmati rice and you can make this fancy if serving to guests by offering optional toppings to add to their bowls of curry such as additional raisins, coconut flakes, mango, fresh cilantro and plain unsweetened yogurt to finish it off.

TURMERIC DUSTED
ROASTED CAULIFLOWER

Serves 2-4

In my opinion, there is nothing better than roasted cauliflower. I absolutely love it and dusting it with turmeric adds extra nutrition and anti-inflammatory benefits. This recipe is so easy to make and can be paired with just about anything. Sometimes we do vegan rice bowls with fresh herbs, seeds and dried fruit. It can also be served as a side dish with your favorite meat, tossed with pasta, or together with any type of curry dish.

1 head cauliflower, washed, cored and chopped
3 tbs extra virgin olive oil
1 tsp sea salt
Freshly ground black pepper
2 tbs turmeric powder

Preheat oven to 400°F.

Place a sheet of parchment paper on a large sheet pan. Spread the chopped cauliflower evenly on the sheet pan then drizzle over the olive oil. Sprinkle with salt, pepper and turmeric. Roast for 30-35 minutes until golden brown, then serve.

RAINBOW SWISS CHARD WITH POMEGRANATE AND APPLE CIDER

Serves 2-4

This is such a simple recipe and yet so incredibly flavorful. The sweet pomegranate seeds paired with the apple cider really make this a fabulous side dish. This would be great with vegetarian rice bowls, pork tenderloin or any cut of meat or fish. It is especially delicious when Swiss chard and apple cider are in season in the fall.

2 tbs coconut oil
2 garlic cloves, peeled and chopped
2 bunches rainbow Swiss chard, washed, chopped and ends removed
1 cup pomegranate seeds
2 tbs apple cider vinegar
1 tbs fresh lemon juice
1 cup fresh apple cider
1 tsp sea salt
Freshly ground black pepper

Heat the coconut oil in a large skillet over a medium heat. Once the coconut oil has melted add the garlic. Let the garlic infuse the oil for 2-3 minutes, then add the Swiss chard. Sauté for 3-4 minutes, then add the pomegranate seeds, apple cider vinegar, lemon juice, apple cider, salt and pepper. Cook approx. 8 minutes until the Swiss chard begins to wilt and is just tender. Serve hot.

SQUASH AND SWEET POTATO BAKE

Serves 2-4

Eating seasonally can provide a lot of value to our health and this dish really highlights all the beautiful squash and sweet potatoes available in the fall season. We often have this as a side dish for Thanksgiving. I have also used it to top a Shepard's pie before and as a side for any of my favorite fish or meat dishes. It is even fabulous as a main dish with roasted vegetables too.

2 sweet potatoes, washed
1 whole acorn
  squash, washed,
2 tbs cultured butter
½ cup low sodium vegetable
  or chicken stock
2 tbs real maple syrup
1 tsp sea salt
Freshly ground black pepper

Preheat your oven to 400°F.

Wash your sweet potatoes, fork prick and then place on an oven-safe cookie sheet. Cut the acorn squash in half, then remove the seeds. Place on the cookie sheet together with the sweet potatoes. Bake for 60 minutes then remove and let cool slightly. Make sure to leave your oven on.

Scoop out the flesh of the sweet potato and acorn squash into a large bowl. Add the butter, stock, maple syrup, salt and pepper. Use a fork or an electric beater. Mash or beat on medium speed then high until the squash and sweet potato are smooth and whipped well. Season with additional salt and pepper. Add the mixture to an oven-safe casserole dish, bake for 20-30 minutes until golden brown then serve.

EMPOWERFUL

SPROUTED QUINOA BOWLS
WITH HERB ROASTED VEGGIES

Serves 2-4

Sprouted grains are so good for our health and the combination of the quinoa with all these delicious roasted veggies and herbs is so delicious and comforting. The quinoa can be cooked on the stove top or in a rice cooker. If you use a rice cooker, simply add the same ratio for quinoa and water and follow your rice cooker's directions for cooking.

2 cups sprouted quinoa
2 cups water
Juice of 1 orange

2 carrots, washed, peeled and sliced into matchsticks
1 pint cherry tomatoes, washed and sliced into halves
1 orange sweet pepper, washed, cored and sliced
2 Portobello mushrooms, washed and sliced
1 red onion, peeled and sliced
4 garlic cloves, peeled and smashed
½ head cauliflower, washed and chopped
2 tbs fresh parsley, washed and chopped
1 tbs dried oregano
1 tbs herbs de Provence
1 tsp sea salt
Freshly ground black pepper
2 tbs extra virgin olive oil
1 package (1oz) gluten-free tamari almonds

Preheat oven to 450°F.

FOR THE QUINOA:
In a medium-sized pot, add the quinoa and water together with a pinch of salt. Place lid on pot and cook over a medium heat. Bring to the boil then reduce heat to low and continue to cook for approx. 30 minutes until the quinoa is fully cooked through. Do not remove the lid but remove from the heat and let sit for 10-15 minutes. Then fork fluff and squeeze the orange juice over the quinoa. Use the fork to toss the orange juice thoroughly through the quinoa then set aside.

FOR THE ROASTED VEGETABLES:
On a large sheet pan, evenly distribute the carrots, tomatoes, peppers, mushrooms, onion, garlic and cauliflower. Sprinkle the vegetables with the parsley, oregano, herbs de Provence, salt, pepper and olive oil. Roast in the oven for 30-35 minutes until all the veggies are golden brown and tender.

Remove from the oven and place one cup of cooked quinoa in a serving bowl. Add a full cup's portion of the roasted veggies, making sure to add any drippings from the veggies. Sprinkle with a few tamari almonds and a small drizzle of olive oil. Serve immediately.

ETHIOPIAN STYLE RED LENTILS
WITH CUMIN AND CINNAMON

Serves 2-4

This is a lovely vegetarian dish that has so many fantastic spices which makes it very unique. It is also very simple to prepare and comes together quickly. Like any stew, the more time it has to rest the better it will be as the flavors can come together. We love to fancy ours up with cilantro garnish, coconut plain yogurt and sweet dried raisins to give it that extra flair. This can be served on its own or over rice.

2 cups red lentils
2 tbs extra virgin olive oil
1 onion, peeled and minced
2 tbs fresh cilantro,
    washed and minced
3 garlic cloves, peeled
    and minced
1 tbs fresh ginger, peeled
    and minced
¼ tsp ground cloves
½ tsp mild yellow
    curry powder
½ tsp ground cardamom
½ tsp ground cumin
1 tsp smoked paprika
½ tsp freshly grated nutmeg
1 tsp cinnamon
3 cups low sodium chicken
    or vegetable stock
Pinch sea salt
Freshly ground black pepper
2 tbs fresh cilantro,
    to garnish

Wash the lentils then set aside briefly. Heat the olive oil in a large stock pot over a medium heat. Add the onion and cook approx. 8 minutes until translucent, then add the cilantro, garlic, ginger, clove, curry powder, cardamom, cumin, paprika, nutmeg and cinnamon. Cook 2-3 minutes so the flavors can come together then add the lentils. Sauté for 1 minute more, then add the stock, salt and pepper. Increase the heat to high so the stew can come to a quick boil, then reduce to low and continue cooking with the top on for 30 minutes. Serve with fresh herb cilantro garnish and sweet raisins.

TIKKA MASALA RED LENTIL CURRY

Serves 2-4

This is such a delicious curry that can be adapted to be made with chicken. We love to serve ours with steamed basmati rice and then top it with mango chutney, raisins and fresh cilantro. This comes together very quickly and yet it tastes like the most delicious slow-cooked comfort food.

2 tbs ghee
1 onion, peeled and diced
1 leek, washed and minced
2 tbs fresh ginger, peeled and minced
1 tbs fresh turmeric, peeled and minced
3 garlic cloves, peeled and minced
2 tsp Ceylon cinnamon
2 tbs cumin
2 tbs smoked paprika
Pinch of sea salt
Freshly ground black pepper
2 cups fresh spinach, washed
2 potatoes, washed, peeled and diced
1 cup fresh or frozen peas
2 cups red lentils, washed
12oz crushed tomatoes
3 tbs coconut cream
2 cups low sodium vegetable or chicken stock

Heat the ghee in a large stock pot over a medium heat. Once the ghee has melted, add the onion, leek, ginger, turmeric and garlic. Cook approx. 8 minutes until translucent, then add 1 tsp of the cinnamon, 1 tbs of the cumin and 1 tbs of the smoked paprika. Cook for 2 minutes so the flavors can come together, then add the salt and pepper. Now add the spinach, potatoes, peas and red lentils. Sauté for 2 minutes, then immediately add the tomatoes, coconut cream and stock. Add the remaining cinnamon, cumin and smoked paprika. Increase the heat to high briefly until the lentils come to a quick boil, then immediately reduce to low and place the top on the pot. Cook approx. 15 minutes so the flavors can come together and the potatoes are fork tender. Add additional stock if the curry becomes too thick. Serve hot with crusty bread or on a bed of rice.

⚡   VEGETARIAN

05

—FISH + SEAFOOD

'Stepping into your truth is really just about uncovering
what makes you uniquely you. When we honor this,
life just begins to flow.'

—CHEF EMERY

ASPARAGUS WRAPPED IN SMOKED SALMON FILLED WITH GOAT CHEESE, LEMON AND FRESH HERBS

Serves 2-4

This delicious dish will have you looking like the super star of your next dinner party or get-together with friends. This perfect hors d'oeuvre can be grain free or can be served with your favorite gluten-free cracker for some extra crunch!

---

2 soft Medjool dates, pitted
¼ cup raw walnuts
1 tsp sea salt
1lb fresh asparagus, washed
1 (4oz) container of herb goat cheese (preferably local, if possible)
Zest of 1 Meyer lemon or regular lemon
1 tbs fresh Meyer lemon juice
1 bunch of fresh mint, washed
6oz wild-caught smoked salmon, sliced

In a small bowl, soak the dates and raw nuts in water for at least 5-10 minutes. Once softened, discard the water, remove the walnuts and dates, and set aside.

Fill a medium-sized pot with water and add the salt. Place the heat on high and bring to a boil. Add the asparagus and cook no longer than 3 minutes. Transfer the asparagus to an ice bath to cool completely. Once cooled, cut the ends off the asparagus and set aside.

In a food processor, add the goat cheese, lemon zest, lemon juice, two sprigs of fresh mint, and the softened dates and walnuts. Pulse continually until the ingredients are fully combined and form a smooth paste. Set aside.

On a large plate assemble the smoked salmon slices. Using a butter knife or spatula, add a dollop of the goat cheese filling to each slice. Then add one asparagus along with a sprig of fresh mint. Fold the salmon slices over like a blanket and repeat until your plate is full. A gluten-free cracker can be added underneath to make this a canapé or keep it grain free.

Asparagus can be substituted for fresh endive leaves which would also be absolutely delicious. Simply add a dollop of goat cheese into the center of an endive leaf along with the mint and then roll the smoked salmon inside. If using endive leaves, do not blanch the leaves. Simply wash and use them fresh.

PAN SEARED HALIBUT

Serves 2-4

Crispy shallots honestly make any dish look fancy and taste absolutely fantastic. This dish comes together very quickly and will give dinner that professional look with minimal effort.

For the Halibut:
1-1.5 lbs wild-caught
    fresh halibut
Pinch of sea salt
Freshly ground black pepper
1 tbs fresh parsley,
    washed and minced
1 tbs extra virgin olive oil

For the Potatoes:
4-5 medium-sized red
potatoes, washed and
    sliced into wedges
2 shallots, peeled and sliced
3 garlic cloves, peeled
    and sliced
1 tbs herbs de Provence
1 tbs fresh parsley,
    washed and chopped
1 tbs fresh chives, washed
    and chopped
1 tsp sea salt
Freshly ground black pepper
2 tbs extra virgin olive oil

Preheat your oven to 450°F.

Wash your halibut, place on a plate, then season both sides of the fish with the salt, pepper, parsley and oil. Cover and set aside temporarily in the fridge.

Arrange the potato wedges on a large sheet pan. Add the shallots and garlic, then sprinkle the entire sheet pan with the herbs de Provence, parsley, chives, salt and pepper. Drizzle with a little olive oil then roast in the oven for 35-40 minutes until the potatoes and shallots are crispy and golden brown. Halfway through the cooking time, take a wooden spatula and move around the potatoes, shallots and fresh herbs so that they cook evenly.

Remove the fish from the fridge and let come to room temperature for 5 minutes. Add the olive oil to a large sauté pan and place over a medium heat. Let the pan get nice and hot then add the halibut. Cook approx. 5 minutes on each side, then flip with a spatula. Each side should be slightly golden brown. Once cooked, serve immediately with roasted potatoes, crispy shallots and a big salad.

SHRIMP TACOS WITH MANGO SALSA

Serves 2-4

These tacos are so light and fresh and can be really jazzed up with all the fixings or kept simple. The sweetness of the mango paired with the cumin and chili powder gives an exotic twist to this easy-to-prepare meal. You can peel and devein the shrimp yourself or you can purchase shrimp that has already been peeled and deveined.

1½ lbs wild-caught
large shrimp, peeled
and deveined
2 tbs extra virgin olive oil
1 tsp sea salt
Freshly ground black pepper
1 tbs garlic, peeled
and minced
2 tbs fresh cilantro,
washed and chopped
1 tsp cumin
1 tsp chili powder
6-8 organic corn tortillas

For the Mango Salsa:
1 mango, washed, pitted
and diced
2 tbs fresh cilantro,
washed and chopped
2 tbs organic red
onion, diced
½ tsp sea salt
Freshly ground black pepper
2 tbs fresh lime juice
½ tsp organic real
maple syrup
1 Jalapeño, washed, seeded
and diced (optional)
1 tbs extra virgin olive oil
1 tbs apple cider vinegar

1 avocado, pit removed,
sliced (optional)
Sour cream or plain
yogurt (optional)
Hot sauce (optional)

Let corn tortillas come to room temperature.

In a medium bowl, add the shrimp, 1 tbs of the olive oil, salt, pepper, garlic, cilantro, cumin and chili powder. Cover and marinate in the fridge for 30 minutes.

Meanwhile, in another bowl, mix together all the mango salsa ingredients. Set aside and let the ingredients come together.

In a medium-sized sauté pan add the remaining 1 tbs of olive oil and place heat on medium to medium/ high. Add the shrimp including the marinade and cook 6-8 minutes. The shrimp will cook very quickly and will be pink in color. Remove from heat.

Place a small sauté pan over a medium heat, add each corn tortilla one at a time for approx. 1 minute until just heated through. Now it is time to assemble. Place two or three corn tortillas on your plate and add a portion of shrimp in the center. Follow with a scoop of mango salsa. You can then add the sliced avocado, hot sauce, and a small tbs of sour cream or plain yogurt.

FISH + SEAFOOD

HADDOCK AND LOBSTER CHOWDER

Serves 2-4

I worked on this recipe awhile to get it just right and I honestly will never change it. This is a cherished dish in our house and we generally save it for special occasions or holidays but, trust me, there is no wrong time to have it. Sometimes I will make this the day before I plan on serving it. This specific chowder just gets better and better the more the stew can come together. If I plan to do that, I will let it cool then move it to a glass container with a lid and refrigerate overnight, then reheat on low the following day.

2 tbs grass-fed butter
1 onion, peeled and diced
2 tbs herbs de Provence
2 celery stalks, washed and diced
1 large bulb fennel, washed and diced
3 bottles clam juice
¾ (32oz) container of low sodium chicken stock
3 tbs cornstarch
5 potatoes, washed, peeled and diced
Pinch of sea salt
Freshly ground black pepper
2¾ lbs fresh haddock
2 containers fresh lobster, chucked
16oz heavy cream

Melt the butter in a large stock pot over a medium heat. Add the onion and herbs de Provence and cook approx. 8 minutes until the onion is translucent. Add the celery and fennel and continue to cook for another 5 minutes until the vegetables are tender.

Add the clam juice, chicken stock and cornstarch. I generally recommend taking the cornstarch and whisking it or placing it in the blender with one of the bottles of clam juice to prevent lumps. Add the potatoes, salt and pepper and increase the heat to high. Once the chowder just begins to boil immediately reduce the heat to low.

Add the fresh haddock and lobster, place the lid on the stock pot and cook approx. 20 minutes until the fish becomes firm. Avoid stirring the chowder so the fish is not broken up. Add the heavy cream and continue to cook on low for another 10 minutes. Turn the heat off and let the flavors come together for another 30 minutes if possible.

Serve hot with crusty bread, toast points and/or a salad.

HADDOCK OVER CORN SALAD

Serves 2-4

This is a really nice dish, especially in the summer when poblano peppers and corn are at their peak seasonally. Any firm, mild white fish (such as flounder or halibut) can be used and the combination of the light fish over this sweetcorn salad is delicious.

For the Fish:
2.5lbs of fresh haddock
3 tbs extra virgin olive oil
Juice of 1 lemon
½ cup white wine
1 tsp sea salt
Freshly ground black pepper

For the Corn Salad:
4 ears fresh corn or
    1½ cups frozen corn
2 poblano peppers,
    washed (optional)
2 tbs extra virgin olive oil
½ onion, peeled and minced
2 garlic cloves, peeled
    and minced
2 tbs chili powder
¼ cup peanuts
3 tbs fresh cilantro,
    washed and minced
Sea salt
Freshly ground black pepper

Preheat oven to 425°F.

Cut all the fresh corn off the cob and add to a large bowl, then set aside briefly. Place the poblano peppers over an open flame on your stove top. If you do not have a gas stove, omit this step and simply deseed, slice and add the poblanos to the bowl. Once you place the pepper over the flame, allow the peppers to roast on each side for 2-3 minutes until they become black. Remove from heat and let cool. Once cool, remove the seeds and outer skin, then dice and add to the bowl with the corn. Set aside briefly.

Heat the olive oil in a large skillet over a medium heat. Add the onion and cook until translucent then add the garlic, chili powder, corn, poblanos, peanuts, cilantro, salt and pepper. Sauté for 5 minutes until all the flavors come together. Set aside briefly.

Place the fish in a medium-sized oven-safe casserole dish. Drizzle with the olive oil, lemon juice, white wine, salt and pepper. Bake 15-20 minutes until the fish is firm.

Once the fish is cooked, add a portion of corn salad to a plate then arrange a piece of fish over the top of the salad. Serve immediately.

SPROUTED QUINOA RICE BOWLS WITH SHRIMP AND FRIED GARLIC

Serves 2-4

Quinoa bowls are a fun twist on the traditional rice bowl. They can be filled with just about anything to keep everyone in your family happy. The sautéed shrimp with the combination of fried garlic and sliced almonds gives this specific recipe a fancy twist that everyone will love. Quinoa can also be done in your rice cooker. Simply follow your rice cooker's directions.

For the Shrimp:
1 tbs extra virgin olive oil
4 garlic cloves, peeled and minced
1 tsp red chili pepper
3 tbs fresh parsley, washed and chopped
1 tsp sea salt
Freshly ground black pepper
1-1.5lbs wild-caught shrimp, shelled and deveined

For the Quinoa:
2 cups low sodium chicken stock or homemade stock
1 tbs extra virgin olive oil
Pinch of sea salt
2 cups sprouted quinoa
½ cup sliced almonds

In a medium-sized pot, over a medium heat, add the chicken stock, olive oil and salt. Add the sprouted quinoa and place the lid on the pot. Allow the quinoa to come to a boil then reduce heat to low and continue to cook for approx. 25 minutes until the quinoa is fully cooked. Remove from heat and wait 5 more minutes, then fork fluff and add the sliced almonds. Place the lid back on and set aside temporarily.

Add the olive oil to a large sauté pan over a medium heat. Add the garlic, red chili pepper, parsley, salt and pepper. Cook for 2 minutes until the garlic begins to fry, then add the shrimp. Continue stirring rapidly and cook for an additional 5-6 minutes until the shrimp are just cooked through and pink in color. Serve over sprouted quinoa with pan juices. Plates can be garnished with additional fresh parsley and freshly ground black pepper.

MISO PAINTED WILD-CAUGHT SALMON

Serves 2-4

This is a favorite in our house and the combination of the miso paired with the honey and soy sauce really gives the fish a special flair. I like the versatility of it as well as you can bake the fish in the oven or put it on your grill in the summertime. We generally love it with rice, mashed or roasted potatoes, or parsnips and a big salad.

---

4 wild-caught salmon fillets (you can ask your fish store to cut the fish into individual portions)
2 tbs extra virgin olive oil
2 tbs raw honey
3 tbs low-sodium gluten-free tamari
2 tbs sweet miso paste
Pinch of sea salt
Freshly ground black pepper

Preheat your oven to 400°F or place your grill on medium/high.

Place your salmon fillets in an oven-safe dish or on a plate if you're grilling outside. Drizzle with olive oil then set aside briefly.

In a small bowl, whisk the honey, tamari and miso paste with a fork. Take a spatula and baste each salmon fillet generously with the miso mixture, then sprinkle with salt and pepper. Bake for 15-20 minutes depending on how well done you like your fish. For the grill, place on the grill for the same amount of time.

MUSSELS WITH WHITE WINE AND GARLIC

Serves 2-4

This is one of my son's favorite things to eat. We are very blessed to have access to the most amazing local mussels here in Maine. This meal comes together very quickly and is quite versatile as it can be served over linguini or with a crusty baguette to dip in the fabulous garlic broth.

---

2 lbs fresh mussels
2 tbs cultured butter
2 tbs extra virgin olive oil
5 garlic cloves, peeled and chopped
3 tbs fresh parsley, washed and chopped
Pinch of sea salt
Freshly ground black pepper
2 (8oz) bottles of fresh clam juice
1 cup white wine

Take a large bowl and wash the mussels well to remove any excess grit or dirt and briefly set aside. Discard any mussels that are open (do not eat them). In a large stock pot over a medium heat, add the butter and olive oil. Once the butter is melted, add the garlic, parsley, salt and pepper, and cook approx. 5 minutes, making sure not to burn your garlic.

Add your mussels and toss well through the garlic mixture, then add the clam juice and white wine. Place the lid on the pot and cook 8-10 minutes until the mussels open up. Serve immediately.

POACHED HADDOCK OVER
ROASTED SWEET POTATOES

Serves 2-4

This meal is an example of how real food when sourced well does not need a complicated recipe to taste absolutely delicious. It is also proof that we can make quick dinners that can elevate our health as well as our taste buds. Any firm white fish (such as flounder or halibut) can be used for this dish.

For the Fish:
1-1.5lbs wild-caught haddock
1 bulb fresh fennel, washed and chopped
4 tbs fresh dill, washed and chopped
1 tsp herbs de Provence
1 tsp sea salt
Freshly ground black pepper
Juice of 1 lemon
1 tbs extra virgin olive oil

For the Roasted
Sweet Potatoes:
2 sweet potatoes, washed, peeled and cut into wedges
2 shallots, washed, peeled and chopped
1 tsp sea salt
Freshly ground black pepper
2 tbs extra virgin olive oil

Preheat oven to 425°F.

Place the fish in a medium-sized oven-safe casserole dish. Sprinkle with the fennel, dill, herbs de Provence, salt and pepper. Add the lemon juice and olive oil. Set aside briefly.

Add the sweet potato wedges to an oven-safe sheet pan (make sure to evenly distribute them). Add the shallots, salt and pepper, then drizzle the olive oil evenly over the potatoes.

Place your sweet potatoes in the bottom part of your oven and set your timer for 20 minutes. When the timer goes off, move the sweet potatoes around the pan with a spatula so they can evenly cook. Leave the sweet potatoes in the oven and now add your fish to the top part of your oven. Set your timer for an additional 15 minutes. Once the timer goes off, the fish should be perfectly cooked and your sweet potatoes should be crispy and delicious. Serve immediately.

WILD-CAUGHT SALMON KEBABS WITH VEGGIES

Serves 2-4

Delicious would be an understatement for this dish and it is surprisingly easy to make. This is a perfect example of how real food does not need a lot of ingredients to be absolutely incredible. Veggies can be altered and changed depending on the season.

1-1.5lbs wild-caught salmon (ask your fish store to cube the fish for you for kebabs)
1 container cherry tomatoes
1 red onion, peeled and quartered
1 package mini Portobello mushrooms
1 yellow pepper, washed, deseeded and cut
1 head cauliflower, washed and cut
1 tsp sea salt
Freshly ground black pepper
2 tbs extra virgin olive oil
1 package wooden bbq skewers

Preheat oven to 475°F or outdoor grill to high.

Cut all your veggies and fish so that they can be assembled onto skewers. Alternate each skewer with the fish, tomatoes, onion, mushrooms, peppers and cauliflower. Keep repeating until all the ingredients have been used up. If using your oven, place all the skewers onto a large sheet pan then drizzle with olive oil, salt and pepper, and place in the oven for 20-25 minutes until both the fish and veggies are fully cooked. Halfway through the cooking time, use tongs to flip the skewers over so that they can evenly cook.

If using a grill, once the skewers are assembled drizzle with olive oil, salt and pepper, then place on the grill and cook approx. 8 minutes on each side (turn the grill down to medium if it is too hot), using tongs to flip them.

Serve with rice or on their own with a big salad.

WILD-CAUGHT SALMON WITH CRISPY SAGE OVER GARLIC BUTTERMILK MASHED POTATOES

Serves 2-4

This is another really easy dish to put together. The combination of the salmon over this buttermilk mashed potato recipe is divine. My kids will honestly eat anything that is paired with these mashed potatoes.

Mashed Potatoes
for the Salmon:
4 portions wild-caught salmon (ask your fish store to cut the fish into individual portions)
1 bunch fresh sage, washed and leaves torn off
2 tbs extra virgin olive oil
1 tbs local raw honey
1 tsp herbs de Provence
1 tsp sea salt
Freshly ground black pepper

For the Mashed Potatoes:
4 Yukon gold organic potatoes, washed, peeled and cut into pieces
2 garlic cloves, peeled and chopped
1½ tbs cultured grass-fed butter
1 tsp sea salt
Freshly ground black pepper
¾ cup buttermilk
1 tbs fresh chives, washed and chopped
1 lemon, washed and cut into wedges

Preheat your oven to 450°F.

Place the salmon in a large oven-safe fish dish or casserole dish (skin sides down). Sprinkle the fish with the sage then drizzle with the olive oil, honey, herbs de Provence, salt and pepper. Set aside briefly.

Take a large stock pot with a lid and fill with cold water and add a pinch of sea salt. Add the potatoes to the pot along with the garlic. Place the lid on and turn the heat on your stove top to high. Let the water begin to boil then reduce heat to medium, sliding the lid off slightly to the side so the steam can be released. Cook the potatoes approx. 30 minutes until tender.

Place your fish in the oven and cook approx. 20 minutes until the salmon is cooked and the sage is crispy.

While the fish is cooking, use the lid to strain the water off of the potatoes (leave the garlic). Quickly add the butter, salt and pepper. Now add the buttermilk and either use a fork or a hand-held mixer to mash the potatoes. If using a mixer, slowly increase the speed up to medium-high and whip the potatoes quickly until they are nice and smooth (you can add more buttermilk if needed). Once the potatoes are whipped, add the chives and additional salt and pepper to taste.

When the fish is done remove from the oven. Place approx. one cup of mashed potatoes on each plate then top with a piece of fish. Garnish with more fresh chives (optional), pepper and a squeeze of one lemon wedge.

SHRIMP AND FISH ETOUFFEE

Serves 2-4

My family really loves this dish. It comes together really quickly too which is great because it tastes like you've spent a lot of time in the kitchen when you haven't.

2 tbs extra virgin olive oil
1 yellow onion, peeled
    and minced
Freshly ground black pepper
Pinch of sea salt
4 garlic cloves, peeled
    and minced
1 tbs dried oregano
4 celery stalks, washed
    and chopped
3 tbs fresh parsley,
    washed and minced
1 cup white wine
2 (8oz) bottles clam broth
24oz crushed tomatoes
2 lbs flounder, haddock
    or firm, mild white fish
1 lb shrimp, peeled,
    deveined and
    tails removed
2 tbs green onions,
    washed and minced
2 cups basmati rice, cooked

Heat the olive oil in a large stock pot over a medium heat. Once hot, add the onions, pepper and salt and cook approx. 8 minutes until the onions are translucent. Add the garlic, oregano, celery and parsley, and continue to cook approx. 5 more minutes. Stand back slightly and add the white wine to deglaze the pan, stir with your spoon then add the clam broth and crushed tomatoes. Season with salt and pepper, then add the fish and shrimp.

Cook 10-15 minutes until the fish is firm and the shrimp is pink. Add the cooked rice to the pot. Let all the flavors come together. Serve in bowls and garnish with freshly minced green onions.

06

—MEAT DISHES

'I used to forget that every day was a choice. Every day
we can choose it. Perception is a decision. I always want
to lean back into love, this is how we change the world.'

—CHEF EMERY

SWEET ITALIAN SAUSAGES WITH SAUTÉED ONIONS AND PEPPERS

Serves 2-4

This dish is generally loved by all and is very versatile. It can be served with lacto-fermented sauerkraut as well, for gut health, along with some Dijon mustard.

4-6 pasture-raised sweet Italian sausages (chicken or vegetarian sausages can be substituted)
2 tbs extra virgin olive oil
2 yellow onions, peeled and sliced
1 tsp sea salt
Freshly ground black pepper
2 green peppers, washed, cored and sliced
1 jar lacto-fermented sauerkraut
1 jar Dijon mustard

In a large pot, add water and the sausages. Place the lid on the pot and cook over a medium heat. Let the water come to a boil then reduce heat to medium-low and cook for approx. 30 minutes. Remove from the heat once cooked and pour the water off. Take each sausage and slice lengthwise in half, then set aside temporarily.

Heat the olive oil in a large sauté pan over a medium heat. Add the onions, salt and pepper. Cook for approx. 10 minutes until the onions are translucent and begin to brown. Add the peppers and continue to cook for an additional 10 minutes until the peppers are tender. Add the sliced sausages and cook until the sausages are slightly browned.

Take a plate and add a generous portion of onions and peppers, then top with the sliced sausages. Grind more fresh ground black pepper and serve with lacto-fermented sauerkraut and Dijon mustard.

INSTAPOT PORK AND PINEAPPLE

Serves 2-4

The instapot can be a really valuable time-saving tool in the kitchen. One of the many things that I really love about it is that it literally presses and infuses the broth or stock with whatever you put in it. I really like to utilize it as an opportunity to jam-pack a lot of nutrition and a variety of plant species into a meal as the pressure literally presses it into your food. This is a great way to optimize your health while eating something absolutely delicious. You can also substitute pork chops, bone-in or boneless.

---

1 ham shoulder or
    medium-sized ham steak
1 shallot, peeled
    and chopped
1 red onion, peeled
    and chopped
3 garlic cloves, peeled
2 tbs fresh ginger, minced
1 apple washed, cored
    and sliced
2 tbs fresh parsley,
    washed and minced
2 tbs herbs de Provence
1 tbs dried oregano
Pinch of sea salt
Freshly ground black pepper
1 tbs dried mustard seeds
1 tbs dried coriander seeds
3 tbs fish sauce
2 tbs gluten-free low
    sodium tamari
1 small can diced
    pineapple with the juice

Place the ham into the pot along with the shallot, onion, garlic, ginger and apple, making sure to arrange them evenly around the meat. Add the parsley, herbs de Provence, oregano, salt, pepper, mustard seeds, coriander seeds, fish sauce, tamari and the diced pineapple with the juice.

Place the top on your instapot and make sure the valve is on sealing. Cook on manual pressure for 45 minutes. Let rest for 20 minutes, then release steam, making sure to stand back so you do not get burned. I generally put a kitchen cloth over the steam valve as it's releasing. Remove the ham from the pot and cut into pieces, set aside briefly. We serve ours over gluten-free ramen noodles or over rice bowls. Place your noodles or rice into each bowl, add the ham pieces, then ladle the broth and pineapple on top and serve.

ASIAN-MARINATED FLANK STEAK

Serves 2-4

This is a family staple in our house. This recipe is so good and takes steak to another level. It is one of my kids' favorite meals and it is especially fantastic on the grill in the summer. We love this with a big salad on a warm summer night or served with baked or mashed potatoes in the winter.

---

1 flank steak
2 garlic cloves, peeled
2 tbs fresh ginger, sliced
Juice of 1 orange
½ cup gluten-free low
    sodium tamari
¼ cup raw local honey
Pinch of sea salt
Freshly ground black pepper

Place the flank steak in a large glass container with a lid. Sprinkle the garlic and ginger over the steak. In a small bowl, add the orange juice, tamari, honey, salt and pepper. Whisk well, pour it over the steak and then place the lid on the container. Give it a good shake then place in the fridge to marinate for at least 1-2 hours. Ideally overnight, if possible.

Once ready to cook, place your grill on high. Once hot, transfer the steak to the grill. Cook over a high heat for approx. 5 minutes on each side, only flipping the steak once (longer if you like your steak more well done). Remove from the grill and let rest for 5 minutes, then slice at an angle following the grain of the steak. Serve with salad or potatoes.

EMPOWERFUL

⚡ MEAT DISHES

MAPLE-GLAZED PORK TENDERLOIN

Serves 2-4

This is a regular in our house. The unique combination of the spices paired with the sweetness of the cinnamon and maple syrup will make your whole house smell divine. We serve this a number of ways. It's fantastic with garlic mashed potatoes, rice or a sprouted lentil mix.

---

1 tbs chili powder
1 tbs dried cumin
1 tbs Ceylon cinnamon
1 tsp sea salt
Freshly ground black pepper
1 pork tenderloin
2 tbs extra virgin olive oil
3 garlic cloves, peeled
    and minced
3 tbs real maple syrup
1 cup low sodium
    chicken stock

Preheat oven to 425°F.

In a small bowl, add the chili powder, cumin, cinnamon, salt and pepper. Use a fork to combine the spices, then rub your pork tenderloin generously with the spice mixture.

Add the olive oil to a large oven-safe cast-iron pan or pot with a lid and place over a medium heat. Once hot, add the pork tenderloin. Cook approx. 5 minutes on each side until golden brown. Once browned, sprinkle the minced garlic over the tenderloin then quickly pour the maple syrup over too. Cook approx. 2 minutes then add the chicken stock.

Remove from heat then place the lid on. Immediately place the pot in the oven and cook approx. 20 minutes. Once cooked, remove from oven. Let the tenderloin rest for 10 minutes so the flavors can come together. Slice vertically and use the pan drippings to spoon over the tenderloin.

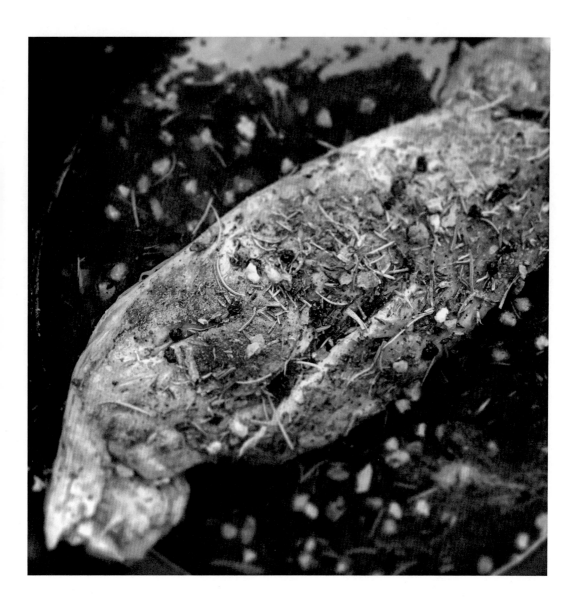

HOMEMADE SLOPPY JOES

Serves 2-4

Everybody loves these and they are so quick to come together as well as being super satisfying when you're seeking comfort food. We pile ours high on sprouted rolls or gluten-free bread. It's fabulous over pasta too!

1 tbs extra virgin olive oil
1 onion, peeled and minced
1lb ground grass-fed beef
    or ground turkey
2 garlic cloves, peeled
    and minced
12oz strained crushed
    tomatoes or 1 jar
    of marinara
2 tbs ketchup
1 tbs mustard
1 tbs real maple syrup
Pinch of sea salt
Freshly ground black pepper

Heat the olive oil in a large skillet over a medium heat. Add the onion and cook approx. 8 minutes until translucent. Add the ground beef or turkey and cook an additional 8-10 minutes until the ground meat is well done and fully cooked. Add the garlic and cook for one more minute, then add the tomatoes, ketchup, mustard, maple syrup, salt and pepper. Increase heat to high until it just comes to a subtle boil then immediately reduce to low and cook down for 20 minutes. Serve hot.

CORNED BEEF AND CABBAGE

Serves 2-4

When you source a good quality cut of corned beef, it makes this dish beyond fantastic. In March, our local co-op always carries local corned beef and to say it's delicious is an understatement. I've been making this exact recipe for several years and it honestly is one of the best versions I've ever had. I hope you feel the same.

1lb corned beef
4 garlic cloves, peeled (then use one to rub the meat)
2 tbs extra virgin olive oil
1 onion, peeled and minced
1 shallot, peeled and minced
5 carrots, washed, peeled and diced
5 juniper berries, crushed
1 tbs mustard seeds
5 allspice
2 bay leaves
¾ 32floz low sodium chicken stock
3 cups water
2 tbs real maple syrup
½ cup apple cider vinegar
1 green cabbage, washed, cored and chopped
5-6 large potatoes, washed, peeled and cut

Take the corned beef and rub the outside of it thoroughly with raw garlic. Then set the meat aside briefly and save the garlic. Heat the olive oil in a large stock pot over a medium heat. Once the pot is hot, add the onion and shallot and cook approx. 8 minutes until translucent. Add the carrots, juniper berries, mustard seeds, allspice and bay leaves, then sauté for 5 minutes to release the aromatics.

Add the chicken stock, water, maple syrup, apple cider vinegar and the corned beef to the pot. With the lid on, increase the heat to high and bring to a boil. Reduce to medium, keeping the lid on the pot, and cook approx. 30 minutes. Add the cabbage and potatoes, reduce the heat to low and cook for an additional 30 minutes with the lid on.

Remove the corned beef from the pot and slice on the diagonal. You can use a slotted spoon to remove the mustard seeds, juniper berries, allspice and bay leaves (optional). We believe in our house if you get a bay leaf, it means good luck! Serve a couple of slices of corned beef each into shallow bowls, then use a spoon to add the broth, potatoes, cabbage and carrots.

GRASS-FED LETTUCE WRAP BURGERS WITH SWEET POTATO FRIES

Serves 2-4

Garlic Herb Aioli is honestly divine and can be done in a way that is absolutely delicious and healthy too. This can be altered to be a vegetarian dish simply by substituting your favorite veggie burger recipe. You can also substitute turkey or chicken burgers for those not eating beef.

For the Sweet Potato Fries:
2 sweet potatoes, washed, peeled and sliced
1 tsp sea salt
Freshly ground black pepper
1 tbs herbs de Provence
2 tbs extra virgin olive oil

For the Fresh Herb Garlic Aioli:
3 tbs of vegenaise or avocado mayo
Juice of 1 lemon
¼ tsp real maple syrup
¼ tsp sea salt
Freshly ground black pepper
2 tbs fresh cilantro, washed and minced
1 tbs fresh parsley, washed and minced
1 garlic clove, peeled and minced

For the Burgers:
4 grass-fed beef burgers
4 large pieces of romaine lettuce or iceberg
1 tomato, washed, cored and sliced
1 red onion, peeled and sliced

Preheat oven to 450°F.

Arrange the sliced sweet potatoes on a large sheet pan. Sprinkle with the salt, pepper and herbs de Provence, then drizzle with the olive oil. Bake in the oven for 35-40 minutes until crispy and golden brown. Halfway through the baking time, take a spatula and flip the sweet potatoes so they cook evenly.

In a small bowl, add the vegenaise or avocado mayo, lemon juice, maple syrup, salt, pepper, cilantro, parsley and garlic. Use a spoon to fully combine the ingredients then set aside.

Heat a large sauté pan over a medium-high heat. Add the burgers and cook approx. 8 minutes on each side until cooked.

It's time to assemble! Take a romaine or iceberg lettuce leaf then add a generous tbs of the aioli. Place a burger on top and add all your favorite fixings such as red onion, fresh tomato, a slice of avocado, pickles and lacto-fermented dill pickle sauerkraut just to name a few. Then wrap the lettuce around the burger. Serve with sweet potato fries.

ITALIAN "MEATBALL" SOUP WITH VEGGIES

Serves 2-4

This soup is very satisfying, especially on a cool evening. The meat can be omitted for vegans and vegetarians making it a delicious vegetarian soup. I highly recommend adding whatever seasonal vegetables are available at the time, which makes this soup very versatile. The below vegetables are just suggestions.

3 sweet Italian sausages or chicken sausages
2 tbs extra virgin olive oil
1 onion, peeled and minced
1 tsp sea salt
Freshly ground black pepper
1 tsp herbs de Provence
1 tsp dried oregano
1 celery stalk, washed and chopped
2 carrots, washed, peeled and chopped
1 zucchini, washed and chopped
3 garlic cloves, peeled and minced
1 (18oz) jar diced tomatoes
6 cups low sodium chicken stock or homemade stock

Wash and chop all the veggies you will be using then set aside. Take a sharp knife and remove the outer casing of your sausages, then cut your sausages into bite-size pieces. This is a quick way to give the "idea" of a meatball without going through the steps of making them.

Heat the olive oil in a large stock pot over a medium heat. Add the onion, salt, pepper, herbs de Provence and oregano. Cook approx. 5 minutes until the onions are translucent and beginning to brown. Add the celery and carrots and cook for another 2 minutes.

Add the sausage and continue to cook approx. 8 minutes until the sausage is browned and almost fully cooked through. Continue to use a wooden spoon to sauté the veggies so they do not burn. Add the zucchini and garlic. Cook for an additional 2 minutes. Add the diced tomatoes and chicken stock.

Increase heat to high until the soup almost comes to a boil then reduce to low. Place the lid on and continue to simmer for approx. 30 minutes. Garnish with fresh herbs and serve immediately.

07

—POULTRY

'Find you lane, breath life into it. Let it flow.'
—CHEF EMERY

TURKEY MEATLOAF

Serves 2-4

This is a regular staple in our house. Everyone loves this and I worked on the recipe for a while to get the ratios just right. We usually serve ours with garlic mashed potatoes and lots of veggies. I often double this recipe to make an extra-large loaf.

1lb ground turkey
½ white onion, peeled and minced
1 egg
½ cup gluten-free breadcrumbs or regular breadcrumbs
1 tbs dried oregano
2 tbs ketchup
1 tbs Worcestershire sauce
Pinch of sea salt
Freshly ground black pepper

Preheat oven to 350°F.

Add the ground turkey to a large bowl together with the onion, egg, breadcrumbs, oregano, ketchup, Worcestershire sauce, salt and pepper. Mix well until fully combined.

Grease a bread pan with a little olive oil. Add the meatloaf mixture to the pan, then bake in the oven for 30-45 minutes until firm and golden brown on top.

Chef's tip
If you double the recipe, please allow for one hour of baking time.

LEMONGRASS CHICKEN IN COCONUT CURRY

Serves 2-4

I had to write this recipe down the moment it passed my lips because it was just such a lovely balance of flavors. It tastes like really fabulous take out except you made it at home without all that extra stuff we do not need when eating out. I hope you enjoy this as much as we do in our house.

1lb boneless, skinless chicken, diced
2 garlic cloves, peeled and sliced
3 tbs fresh cilantro, washed and diced
2 green onions, washed and diced
2 tbs fish sauce
1 tbs extra virgin olive oil
1 tsp sea salt
1 tbs dried lemongrass
Freshly ground black pepper
1 tsp unrefined coconut oil
½ tsp mild yellow curry powder
1 large head of broccoli, washed and diced
1 tbs dried lemongrass
3 tbs fresh basil, washed and diced
1 can full-fat coconut milk
2 tbs real maple syrup
2 tbs fish sauce

In a large glass container, preferably with a top, add the chicken, garlic, cilantro, green onions, fish sauce, olive oil, salt, lemongrass and pepper. Use a fork to fully combine the ingredients, then place in your refrigerator to let marinate, ideally for 2 hours but you could also cook the chicken right away (the flavor just won't be as pronounced).

Heat the coconut oil in a large wok over a high heat. Add the marinated chicken and cook for 6-8 minutes until the chicken is firm, then add the curry powder and cook for one more minute. Add the broccoli, lemongrass and fresh basil. Cook for an additional minute, then add the coconut milk, maple syrup and fish sauce. Decrease the heat to low and let simmer for 5 minutes until the broccoli is just tender. Serve immediately with crusty bread or boiled rice.

PEANUT CHICKEN SATAY SKEWERS

Serves 2-4

This recipe will have you dreaming of hot summer days, especially when you do not want to get involved in cooking over a hot stove. I love skewers and grilling because it is so quick, easy and is a snap to clean up. Kids especially enjoy getting involved in a meal like this because they can help. The versatility of this recipe is endless too as you can choose whatever veggies you love or that are in season. This can also be easily adapted for vegans/vegetarians by substituting the chicken for non-GMO organic tofu cubes. We love to serve this dish with a big salad and sometimes some steamed basmati rice.

For the Marinade
½ cup peanut butter
2 tbs fish sauce
¼ cup gluten-free low
   sodium tamari
¼ cup water
2 tbs local raw honey
Pinch of sea salt
Freshly ground black pepper

1lb boneless, skinless
   chicken breast or non-
   GMO tofu, chopped into
   skewer pieces

For the Vegetables
1 large red onion,
   peeled and cut into
   skewer pieces
1 large Vidalia onion,
   peeled and cut into
   skewer pieces
1 zucchini, washed and cut
   into skewer pieces
1 red pepper, washed,
   cored and cut into
   skewer pieces
1 green onion, washed,
   cored and cut into
   skewer pieces
2 Portobello mushrooms,
   washed and cut into
   skewer pieces

For the Extra Peanut Sauce to Drizzle
½ cup peanut butter
½ cup water
2 tbs fish sauce
1 tbs local raw honey
1 lime, washed and cut into
   wedges for serving

Combine the peanut butter, fish sauce, tamari, water, honey, salt and pepper in a medium-sized bowl or a high-speed blender. If using a blender, place speed on high and blend until fully combined. If using a bowl, use a fork to whisk until all the ingredients are combined. Place the chicken into a large airtight container with a top. Using a spatula, pour the peanut satay over the chicken and let marinate for at least 2 hours in the fridge.

Wash and cut all of the veggies into skewer-size pieces then briefly set aside.

In a medium-sized bowl or high-speed blender, add all of the extra peanut sauce ingredients. If using a bowl, whisk with a fork until all the ingredients are well combined then set aside. If using a blender, place all of the ingredients into the blender and place the speed on high until all the ingredients are fully combined. Use a spatula to spoon the mixture out of the blender and set aside.

Preheat your grill to high. Remove your chicken from the refrigerator and begin to assemble your skewers by alternating varying veggies with the chicken (discard the peanut sauce that the chicken was marinated in). Once all your skewers are assembled, place on the grill and cook approx. 10 minutes on each side until the chicken is fully cooked and the veggies are roasted. Depending on your grill, you may need to adjust the temperature to a medium-high heat.

The skewers can be served on their own or with a big salad and/or rice. Drizzle each skewer with additional peanut sauce and a squeeze of fresh lime juice. The extra peanut sauce can be saved in an airtight container for 3-5 days and can be used for a dressing on salads or to dip with spring rolls.

CHICKEN RED CURRY

Serves 2-4

This dish comes together very quickly and everyone loves it in our house because it really tastes like a red curry you might get when eating out. We love to serve this over rice and you can add whatever veggies you want. Fresh broccoli and bamboo shoots are great additions, and it may be surprising but pineapple is actually really yummy as well.

1 tbs extra virgin olive oil
1 garlic clove, peeled
   and minced
1 tbs fresh ginger, peeled
   and minced
1 onion, peeled and minced
1 lb boneless, skinless
   chicken breast, diced
1 tbs fish sauce
3 tbs real maple syrup
1 can full-fat coconut milk
3 tbs red curry paste
½ cup low sodium
   chicken stock

Heat the olive oil in a medium-sized stock pot over a medium heat. Add the garlic, ginger and onion and cook for approx. 8 minutes until the onion is translucent. Add the chicken and continue to cook for an additional 8 minutes until the chicken is firm.

Add the fish sauce, maple syrup, coconut milk, red curry paste and chicken stock. Briefly increase the heat to high, and using a spoon, fully combine all of the ingredients. Immediately reduce the heat to low then place the lid on the pot and cook down for 30 minutes. If you are adding additional veggies, you would do so in the last 10 minutes of cooking time so they are just tender and not overcooked.

MARINATED CHICKEN BURGERS

Serves 2-4

These are super satisfying and can be altered depending on your needs. The marinade works for tofu as well so you can accommodate those that are vegan or vegetarian and you can choose to use the bun or not. Adding your favorite fixings really makes these super delicious. I've added some suggestions to the bottom of this recipe.

---

4 skinless, boneless chicken breasts or non-GMO tofu
4 gluten-free sprouted buns (optional)
1 red onion, peeled and sliced
1 avocado, washed, peeled, pitted and sliced
3 cups salad greens

Marinade for the Chicken Burgers
½ cup apple cider vinegar
½ cup extra virgin olive oil
1 tsp sea salt
Freshly ground black pepper
1 tsp real maple syrup
1 tsp dried oregano
1 tsp herbs de Provence
1 garlic clove, peeled and smashed

Add the chicken breasts to a medium-sized bowl. In a small bowl, whisk the apple cider vinegar, olive oil, salt, pepper, maple syrup, oregano, herbs de Provence and garlic. Pour the marinade over the chicken breasts, cover and let marinate for 30 minutes in the fridge.

Assemble the red onion and avocado on a plate along with the salad greens.

Remove the chicken breasts from the fridge and cook in a large sauté pan together with 2-3 tbs of the marinade over a medium heat. Cook each side for approx. 6 minutes until the chicken browns and is firm.

Turn the heat off and let the chicken rest for just a minute. In the meantime, toast your gluten-free buns, if using. Serve the chicken with your favorite fixings such as dill pickles, ketchup, a touch of avocado mayo, tomato slices, avocado slices, lacto-fermented sauerkraut, micro greens and salad greens just to name a few.

FRESH HERB TURKEY MEATBALLS WITH ROASTED TURMERIC-DUSTED CAULIFLOWER

Serves 2-4

The herbs in the meatballs can be varied, as well as the spices and herbs for the roasted cauliflower. The breadcrumbs can also be omitted, but if you choose to omit them, the meat will have a stickier consistency when forming the meatballs. Vegetarians can omit the meatballs altogether and make rice bowls with the roasted cauliflower.

For the Meatballs:
1lb ground turkey
3 tbs fresh parsley,
    washed and chopped
3 tbs fresh cilantro,
    washed and chopped
1 tsp dried lemongrass
2 tbs fish sauce
½ tsp sea salt
Freshly ground black pepper
1 tsp garlic, peeled
    and minced
1 tsp ginger, washed,
    peeled and minced
1 egg, beaten
½ cup gluten-free
    breadcrumbs
2 tbs extra virgin olive oil

For the Cauliflower:
1 head cauliflower, washed,
    cored and chopped
1 tsp sea salt
Freshly ground black pepper
1 tbs turmeric
1 tsp dried lemongrass
1 tbs extra virgin olive oil

Preheat oven to 425°F.

In a medium-sized bowl, add the ground turkey, parsley, cilantro, lemongrass, fish sauce, salt, pepper, garlic and ginger. Then add the egg and breadcrumbs. Use a spatula or clean hands to fully combine the ingredients. Assemble the meatballs on a plate, making them into approx. 1-inch balls. Once all the meatballs are made, cover and place in the fridge.

Evenly distribute the cauliflower onto a large oven-safe sheet pan. Sprinkle with the salt, pepper, turmeric and dried lemongrass, then drizzle with the olive oil. Place in the oven and set your timer for 30 minutes. Halfway through the baking time, use a spatula to toss the cauliflower so that it evenly cooks.

Heat the 2 tbs of olive oil in a large sauté pan over a medium heat. Add the meatballs, placing them evenly in the pan so you can flip them easily. Cook for approx. 8 minutes on each side, using a spatula to flip them over. They should be fully cooked and golden brown. When your timer goes off for your cauliflower it's time to eat! Serve the roasted cauliflower together with the meatballs on a plate. Cooked basmati or brown rice can be added to this recipe along with pickled ginger to add a special flair.

ROASTED SWEET POTATOES STUFFED WITH FRESH HERBS AND GROUND CHICKEN

Serves 2-4

These stuffed sweet potatoes are super easy to make and are very versatile as they can be adapted for vegetarians and/or vegans as well. You will need one sweet potato per person.

4 sweet potatoes
2 tbs extra virgin olive oil
½ yellow onion, peeled and minced
1 tsp sea salt
Freshly ground black pepper
1 tbs fresh sage, washed and chopped
1 tbs fresh parsley, washed and chopped
1 tsp dried oregano
1 tsp herbs de Provence
2 garlic cloves, peeled and minced
1lb ground chicken
½ cup low sodium chicken stock or homemade stock

Preheat oven to 350°F.

Prick the sweet potatoes with a fork and place on a cookie sheet. Cook 35-40 minutes until tender.

While the sweet potatoes are cooking, heat 1 tbs of the olive oil in a large sauté pan over a medium heat. Add the onion, salt and pepper. Cook approx. 5 minutes until the onion is translucent and beginning to brown. Add the sage, parsley, oregano and herbs de Provence. Add the garlic and ground chicken. If making this vegan or vegetarian, add your favorite veggies instead. Continue to cook the chicken until fully cooked, approx. 8 minutes. Add the stock, reduce the heat to low and continue to cook for an additional 5 minutes.

Remove the sweet potatoes from the oven, take a sharp knife and slice them down the middle. Drizzle over the remaining 1 tbs of olive oil, and season with salt and pepper. Top with ground chicken and fresh herb mixture and serve.

OVEN ROASTED CHICKEN WITH HERBS DE PROVENCE AND ROASTED PARSNIPS WITH CRISPY SHALLOTS

Serves 2-4

This dinner is so satisfying and feels like comfort food yet is so healthy. When we take real food, and enhance it with dried herbs and plants that come from nature, we just feel better.

½ whole chicken, washed
6 parsnips, washed, peeled
  and chopped lengthwise
1 large shallot, peeled
  and sliced
2 tbs herbs de Provence
1 tsp sea salt
Freshly ground black pepper
2 tbs fresh parsley
2 tbs fresh mint
2 tbs extra virgin olive oil
1 tbs real maple syrup

Preheat oven to 375°F.

Place the chicken in the center of a large sheet pan. Arrange the chopped parsnips and shallots around the chicken. Sprinkle the chicken and vegetables with herbs de Provence, salt, pepper, parsley and mint. Drizzle the olive oil and maple syrup over everything, as well as the whole sheet pan. Roast for one hour until crispy and golden brown.

THAI-STYLE CHICKEN
STIR FRY WITH BASIL

Serves 2-4

This is another fabulous dish that tastes like a really good take out. The combination of the crunchy vegetables with the fresh basil gives it a special flair. My son loves broccoli anytime it is sautéed with basil. This dish is also great because it comes together super quick which makes getting dinner on the table fast.

---

2 tbs fish sauce
2 tbs real maple syrup
¾ gluten-free low
   sodium tamari
2 tbs extra virgin olive oil
1 onion, peeled and minced
1 lb chicken, washed
   and diced
2 tbs fresh ginger, peeled
   and minced
3 garlic cloves, peeled
   and minced
½ cup fresh basil, washed
   and loosely chopped
1 head broccoli, washed
   and chopped
1 red pepper, washed,
   cored, deseeded,
   chopped
2 tbs fresh cilantro,
   washed and chopped

Add the fish sauce, maple syrup and tamari to a small bowl. Whisk with a fork and set aside so the flavors can come together.

Heat the olive oil in a large wok over a high heat. Add the onion and cook for approx. 8 minutes until the onion is translucent. Add the chicken, ginger and garlic and continue to cook for approx. 8 minutes until the chicken is nice and firm. Add the basil, broccoli, red pepper and cilantro, then sauté for 5-8 minutes, stirring constantly, until the veggies begin to become tender.

Add the fish sauce/tamari mixture and reduce heat to low. Continue to cook until the vegetables are tender and the chicken is fully cooked and firm.

CHICKEN THIGHS MARINATED WITH DIJON AND FRESH HERBS

Serves 2-4

Roasted cauliflower is so fantastic and there are so many exciting ways to prepare it that can add a lot of variety to your diet. This cauliflower can be served on its own, over sprouted quinoa for vegetarians or paired with delicious roasted chicken thighs like in this recipe.

For the Roasted Cauliflower:
1 head cauliflower, washed, cored and chopped
2 tbs fresh cilantro, washed and chopped
2 tbs fresh green onions, washed and chopped
2 tbs turmeric
1 tsp sea salt
Freshly ground black pepper
2 tbs extra virgin olive oil
3 tbs raw pumpkin seeds
3 tbs dried fruit juice sweetened cranberries

For the Marinated Chicken Thighs:
8 chicken thighs, skins removed if desired
2 tbs Dijon mustard
2 tbs real maple syrup
2 tbs fresh chives, washed and chopped
1 tbs herbs de Provence
1 tsp sea salt
Freshly ground black pepper
1 tbs extra virgin olive oil

Preheat oven to 400°F degrees.

These two dishes can be prepared at the same time and placed in the oven at the same time.

Arrange the sliced cauliflower evenly on a large sheet pan. Sprinkle with the cilantro, green onions, turmeric, salt and pepper. Drizzle with olive oil and place in oven. Roast for approx. 30-35 minutes until golden brown. When finished remove and sprinkle with the cranberries and pumpkin seeds.

Lay all the chicken evenly on another sheet pan (with or without the skin removed). In a small bowl, add the Dijon mustard and maple syrup. Mix well with a fork then take a basting brush (if you do not have one, just use a spoon) and pour the Dijon/maple syrup mixture over each piece of chicken, coating each piece well. Sprinkle each piece of chicken with the chives, herbs de Provence, salt and pepper. Place both dishes in the oven and bake for 30-35 minutes until the chicken is fully cooked.

08

—BAKING

'Cooking and food are windows into the soul.
When open, it's an endless extensions of all
the love and beauty we have within us.'
—CHEF EMERY

DARK CHOCOLATE
ZUCCHINI MUFFINS

Serves 2-4

These muffins are not only a fabulous way to use up zucchini in the summer months but people freak out over them. The chocolate is so lovely and this particular recipe is super moist.

3 eggs
3 tbs extra virgin olive oil
2 tbs unrefined coconut
    oil, melted
1 tsp real vanilla extract
½ cup real maple syrup
1 cup buttermilk
    or hemp milk
2 cups zucchini, washed
    then shredded (press
    the water out with
    a towel)
2 cups gluten-free
    baking flour
1 tsp Ceylon cinnamon
¾ cup unsweetened cocoa
1 tsp sea salt
2 tbs dark chocolate chips

Preheat oven to 375°F.

Crack the eggs into a large bowl, then add the olive oil, melted coconut oil, vanilla extract, maple syrup and buttermilk. Use a fork or spatula to fully combine, then add the shredded zucchini. Fold the zucchini in until fully combined, then set aside briefly.

In a small bowl, combine the flour, cinnamon, cocoa and salt. Transfer to the wet zucchini mixture. Use a fork or spatula to fully combine the dry ingredients in. Add the chocolate chips and fold them through the batter. Grease a one-dozen muffin tin or line with parchment paper muffin liners. Using a large spoon, add the batter to the muffin tin. Bake for 30-35 minutes. Yields approx. 1 dozen.

BANANA RUM
WALNUT BREAD

Serves 2-4

This recipe is a favorite in our home and the combination of the ghee, ripe bananas and rum make it really lovely, not to mention it is super easy to prepare. You will not even taste the rum and any alcohol will cook off so do not worry about it not being appropriate to give to kids.

---

3 tbs grass-fed ghee
3 eggs
1 tsp real vanilla extract
3 ripe bananas, peeled
    and smashed
3 tbs plain coconut yogurt
⅓ cup real maple syrup
2 tbs high-quality
    rum (optional)
Pinch of sea salt
1 tsp Ceylon cinnamon
2½ cups gluten-free
    baking flour
⅓ cup raw walnuts (optional)

Preheat oven to 375°F.

In a large bowl, add the ghee, eggs, vanilla extract, bananas, coconut yogurt, maple syrup, rum and salt. Using a fork, whisk until combined. Add the cinnamon and fold the flour into the batter using your fork. Add the walnuts and combine, then using a spatula pour the batter into a greased bread pan. Bake for 50-60 minutes. Cool and slice.

APPLE BANANA BREAD WITH PECANS, SUNFLOWER SEEDS AND FLAX

Serves 2-4

This nutty, sweet bread is especially delicious with some almond butter and a cup of tea. While I was making this bread, it made me think of this quote that I love by Alice Waters, "It's around the table and in the preparation of food that we learn about ourselves and the world". It truly captures everything I believe about cooking and what it can be. My daughter and I made this bread together and found great pleasure in the measuring, blending, smelling and tasting. There are distinctive bonds formed when we gather to create delicious meals and enjoy them together. It is in this gathering that I believe we find a piece of ourselves, our bond with others and nature. I encourage you to do the same.

---

2 bananas, mashed
½ cup real maple syrup
½ cup applesauce
1 tsp real vanilla extract
3 eggs
3 tbs grass-fed ghee
7 packages or 2 cups of
   gluten-free oatmeal
1 tsp baking powder
Pinch of sea salt
1 tbs Ceylon cinnamon
1 tsp fresh nutmeg, grated
½ cup sunflower seeds
   raw unsalted
½ cup raw pecans
2 tbs flax seeds

Preheat oven to 375°F.

Add the mashed banana, maple syrup, applesauce, vanilla extract, eggs and ghee into a small bowl. Whisk with a fork until fully combined then set aside briefly.

Blend all the oatmeal in a high-speed blender until it forms into flour. Add the oatmeal flour to a large bowl, then add the baking soda, salt, cinnamon and nutmeg. Use a fork to fully combine the ingredients.

Add the oatmeal flour mixture to the wet banana mixture. Gently combine (do not overmix or the bread will become tough), then add the sunflower seeds and pecans (save a few pecans and sunflower seeds for the top of the bread). Gently mix the seeds and pecans through the batter, then transfer the batter to a greased bread pan. Sprinkle flax seeds and additional sunflower seeds and pecans on top. Bake for 50-55 minutes until golden brown.

EMPOWERFUL

PUMPKIN SEED OATMEAL, CHERRIES AND DARK CHOCOLATE CHIP COOKIES

Serves 2-4

The combination of the pumpkin seeds with the dried cherries and dark chocolate gives these cookies a wonderful crunch with a subtle sweetness. I love the versatility of the recipe too as the seeds, dried fruit and chocolate can be adjusted to your liking.

---

2 eggs
1 tbs real vanilla extract
2 tbs grass-fed
  clarified ghee
1 tsp Ceylon cinnamon
3 tbs real maple syrup
½ can pumpkin purée
1 tsp sea salt
1½ cups gluten-free
  baking flour
4 packages gluten-free
  oatmeal cinnamon
  pumpkin seed or
  1 cup oatmeal
2 tbs sweetened naturally
  dried cherries
⅔ cup dark 70%
  chocolate chips

Preheat oven to 350°F.

In a large bowl, combine the eggs, vanilla extract, ghee, cinnamon and maple syrup. Add the pumpkin purée, salt, flour and oatmeal. Combine with a fork, then add the cherries and chocolate chips. Using a large spoon, scoop the cookie dough onto a greased cookie sheet or a cookie sheet lined with parchment paper. Bake for 20-25 minutes until golden brown. Yields approx. 18 cookies.

BANANA PUMPKIN CHOCOLATE CHIP BREAD

Serves 2-4

Fall is absolutely one of my favorite seasons and this banana bread will have your whole house smelling incredible. This recipe is super easy to make and kids love it too. I enjoy a slice in the afternoon with a hot cup of tea, working on slowing my pace down and finding the beauty in the slow down. This time of year, nature is beginning to transition towards winter and we are a part of nature. You may notice feeling more inward or wanting to curl up on the couch with a good book. I encourage you to do so and this recipe is a perfect opportunity to allow yourself that time. There is something about cooking and connecting with real food that just relaxes the mind. The smell and aromas that fill your home are a sensory gift for the soul that truly connect us with ourselves, nature and others. My hope is that you make this recipe and enjoy the fall slow down and all the beauty that nature provides. Enjoy it by yourself, with family or a good friend.

---

1 tsp extra virgin olive oil
7 individual (8oz) packages of gluten-free oatmeal (you decide what flavor) or 2 cups oatmeal
1 tsp sea salt
1 tsp Ceylon cinnamon
1 tsp baking powder
3 tbs grass-fed ghee
1 tsp real vanilla extract
3 eggs
3 bananas, peeled and mashed
½ (15oz) can pumpkin
½ cup real maple syrup
2 tbs rum (optional)
¼ cup 70% dark chocolate chips
1 additional banana, peeled and sliced in half

Preheat your oven to 375°F.

Grease a bread pan with the oil. Add half of the individual packages of oatmeal or the equivalent of 1 cup to a high-speed blender. Blend on high until it forms into flour. Transfer the flour to a small bowl and add the salt, cinnamon, baking powder and the remaining oatmeal (do not process the remaining oatmeal into flour —leave it in its whole form). Set aside briefly.

In a large bowl, add the ghee, vanilla extract, eggs, bananas, puréed pumpkin, maple syrup and rum. Mix with a fork until well combined, then add the flour mixture. Fold the batter until just fully combined, then add the dark chocolate chips.

Using a spatula, add the batter to your bread pan. Arrange the sliced banana on top of the batter then press the banana down gently into the batter. Bake for approx. 1 hour until golden brown.

APPLE SPICE BUNDT CAKE

Serves 4-6

The only problem with this recipe is that you might want to scarf it down in one sitting. My kids adore this especially in the morning or a slice after school. I personally love it in the afternoon with a hot cup of tea. I've purposely incorporated a lot of spices as any time we have the opportunity to add a variety of plant species and spices, our bodies reap the benefits. Did I mention your house will smell divine too?

---

3 apples, washed, peeled,
   cored and sliced
1 tsp Ceylon cinnamon
1 tsp freshly grated nutmeg
3 cups gluten-free
   baking flour
1 tsp sea salt
2 tsp Ceylon cinnamon
1 tsp ground cloves
1 tsp ground ginger
1 tsp ground cardamom
1 tsp freshly grated nutmeg
4 packages of gluten-free
   oatmeal or 1 cup oatmeal
4 eggs
3 tbs coconut oil
½ cup real maple syrup
1 cup buttermilk
1 tsp real vanilla extract

For the Icing (optional):
2 lemons, juiced
1 tsp lemon extract
1 cup confectioner's sugar

Preheat oven to 375°F.

Add the apples, cinnamon and nutmeg to a medium-sized bowl. Roll the apples in the spices then set aside briefly. In another medium-sized bowl, add the flour, salt, cinnamon, clove, ginger, cardamom, nutmeg and oatmeal. Use a fork to combine then set aside briefly. In a large bowl, add the eggs, coconut oil, maple syrup, buttermilk and vanilla extract. Whisk well, then slowly add the flour mixture until fully combined. Using a spatula, fold the sliced apples into your batter. Grease a Bundt cake pan, then use a spatula to pour the batter in. Bake for 1 hour until golden brown.

While your cake is baking, you can make the icing. Add the juice of 2 lemons and the lemon extract to a small bowl. Use a fork or whisk to slowly incorporate the confectioner's sugar until all the ingredients are fully combined.

Once your cake has cooled, drizzle the icing over the top of the cake and serve.

⚡ BAKING

CARROT CAKE MUFFINS

Serves 2-4

These satisfying muffins are jam-packed with carrots as well as a variety of seeds that give them a fantastic crunch paired with the sweetness of the raisins and spices. They are a favorite of mine and I especially love them for breakfast or in the afternoon with a cup of tea.

---

1 banana, peeled
    and mashed
¼ cup extra virgin olive oil
¼ real maple syrup
Pinch of sea salt
1 tbs real vanilla extract
½ cup plain unsweetened
    coconut yogurt
3 carrots, washed, peeled
    and grated
2 tbs chia seeds
1 tbs hemp seeds
1 tbs Ceylon cinnamon
1 tsp ginger
2 cups gluten-free
    baking flour
2 individual packages
    oatmeal or ½
    cup oatmeal
¼ cup raw sunflower seeds
½ cup raisins

Preheat oven to 375°F.

In a large bowl, add the banana and mash with a fork. Add the olive oil, maple syrup, salt, vanilla extract and yogurt. Mix until well combined, then add the grated carrot. Set aside briefly.

In a small bowl, combine the chia seeds, hemp seeds, cinnamon, ginger, flour and oatmeal. Use a fork to mix, then fold into the wet ingredients. Once combined, add the sunflower seeds and raisins. Grease a one-dozen muffin tin or line with parchment paper muffin liners. Spoon the mixture into the muffin tins. Bake for 30-35 minutes until golden brown. Yields approx. 1 dozen.

PUMPKIN BUNDT CAKE

Serves 2-4

This is a variation of the Apple Spice Bundt Cake and I almost didn't include this recipe but I had to because it is equally delicious. It is especially fabulous in the fall when pumpkin is in season, but you can also use a can of pumpkin purée too if you're short on time. If you are trying to be very vigilant with your sugar intake, you can omit the icing.

---

1 small pumpkin or 1 (15oz) can puréed pumpkin
3 cups gluten-free baking flour
1 tsp sea salt
2 tsp Ceylon cinnamon
1 tsp ground cloves
1 tsp ground ginger
1 tsp ground cardamom
1 tsp freshly grated nutmeg
4 packages of gluten-free oatmeal or 1 cup oatmeal
4 eggs
3 tbs unrefined coconut oil
½ cup real maple syrup
1 cup buttermilk
1 tsp real vanilla extract

For the Icing (optional):
2 lemons, juiced
1 tsp lemon extract
1 cup confectioner's sugar

Wash your pumpkin and carefully cut it open. Remove the seeds and bake for one hour at 375°F. Once cooked, remove from oven, let cool, then scoop the flesh of the pumpkin out and set aside. I will often do this step, in advance. If using puréed pumpkin, you can omit this step.

In a medium-sized bowl, add the flour, salt, cinnamon, clove, ginger, cardamom, fresh nutmeg and oatmeal. Use a fork to combine then set aside briefly. In a large bowl, add the eggs, coconut oil, maple syrup, buttermilk, pumpkin and vanilla extract. Whisk well. Slowly add the flour mixture into the wet ingredients until fully combined. Grease a Bundt cake pan, then use your spatula to pour the batter in.

Bake at 375°F for one hour until golden brown.

While your cake is baking, you can make your icing. Add the juice of 2 lemons and the lemon extract to a small bowl. Use a fork or whisk to slowly incorporate the confectioner's sugar until all the ingredients are fully combined.

Once your cake is cooled, drizzle the icing over the top and serve.

BUTTERMILK CORN BREAD

Serves 2-4

This is such an easy recipe and is a great add-on to any meal. We love ours with chili, stews and soups. It's a nice addition when you are having company. Sometimes I will also add freshly sliced jalapeños and/or fresh cilantro to add some kick to it, or a sprinkle of cheddar cheese for a touch of decadence. We personally really like ours simply with a dab of cultured butter.

1½ cups cornmeal
1 cup gluten-free
  baking flour
1 tsp sea salt
3 tbs extra virgin olive oil
2 cups buttermilk
2 eggs
2 tbs real maple syrup,
  raw honey or molasses

Preheat your oven to 375°F.

Add cornmeal, flour and salt to a small bowl. Using a fork, combine the ingredients then set aside briefly. In a large bowl, add the olive oil, buttermilk, eggs and maple syrup. Whisk well then slowly add the dry ingredients, being careful to not overmix the batter.

Once all the ingredients are fully combined, grease a bread pan or shallow oven-safe baking dish and use a spatula to pour the batter into the pan. Bake for 30 minutes until golden brown.

Chef's tip
This recipe can be doubled when serving a larger group. Simply add additional time for baking, approx. 50-60 minutes, total baking time.

OATMEAL CHOCOLATE CHIP
AND ALMOND BUTTER COOKIES

Serves 2-4

These are really delicious and have a lightness about them that I love. They actually could even pass as a breakfast cookie as essentially it is a really good bowl of oatmeal in the shape of a cookie!

1 tsp baking soda
½ tsp sea salt
6 packages (8oz) gluten-free oatmeal or 1½ cups oatmeal
½ cup gluten-free baking flour
½ cup real maple syrup
1 tsp real vanilla extract
1 cup almond butter or nut butter
3 eggs
½ (10oz) package of dark chocolate chips

Preheat oven to 375°F.

In a small bowl, add the baking soda, salt, oatmeal and flour. Set aside briefly.

In a large bowl, add the maple syrup, vanilla extract, almond butter and eggs. Beat with an electric mixer, gradually increasing the speed to high for 5 minutes until the batter is nice and fluffy. Remove the mixer and, using a fork, combine the flour mixture with the cookie dough batter. Once all the flour is combined, fold the chocolate chips in.

Add parchment paper to two cookie sheets. Spoon the cookie batter onto the cookie sheets leaving space in between the cookies. Bake for approx. 20 minutes until golden brown. Remove from the oven and let cool. These can be stored in an airtight container at room temperature for up to three days. Yields approx. one dozen.

MAGIC BARS

Everyone will think these delicious bars are "magic". The combination of the crispy chocolate coating with the cookie bottom is fantastic. They are also incredibly versatile as the almond butter can be replaced with sunflower butter to make it nut-free. The nuts can also be replaced with pumpkin seeds. Sometimes I'll add dried fruit too, such as cranberries or dark dried cherries. I like to use the Equal Exchange brand for the chocolate chips and Qi'a for the oatmeal.

---

1 cup unsweetened
   almond butter
2 tbs unrefined coconut oil
1 tbs local raw honey
1 tsp sea salt
1 cup quinoa flakes
1 cup gluten-free oatmeal
   or ½ cup oatmeal
½ cup raw almonds
   or cashews

For the Chocolate Coating:
½ a bag 70% dark
   chocolate chips
1 tbs unrefined coconut oil

In a medium-sized bowl, add the almond butter, coconut oil, honey, salt, quinoa flakes, oatmeal and almonds. Using your hands, fully combine all of the ingredients. Line an 8-by-8-by-2 baking pan with parchment paper. Press the mixture into the pan until it is evenly distributed. Set aside briefly.

Using a double boiler (or two pots of similar size placed on top of each other), add water to the bottom pot or to the double boiler. Place the other pot on top and add the chocolate chips and coconut oil. Melt the chocolate over a medium-high heat, then reduce heat slightly. Use a spoon or spatula to combine the chocolate with the coconut oil. Once melted, pour evenly over the top of the magic bar mixture.

Place in the fridge for at least one hour. Once firm, remove the magic bars from the pan leaving the parchment paper on the back. Take a very sharp knife and cut into squares. I generally cut this into either 8 or 10 individual bars. Store them in an airtight glass container in the refrigerator with parchment paper layered in between each bar.

⚡   BAKING

"COOKIE DOUGH" POWER BALLS WITH DARK CHOCOLATE CHIPS

Serves 2-4

Any nut butter can be used, though I like to use half peanut butter and half almond butter, and the nuts or seeds can be varied to your liking. Dried fruit can also be added along with the chocolate chips. This easy recipe can be a fun project with kids as they love doing anything with their hands. These also make a fantastic on-the-go snack or afternoon pick-me-up. I will take two in a reusable container for the road or when we go skiing.

1 cup cashew butter, almond butter, sunflower butter, chocolate hazelnut butter or unsalted peanut butter
1 cup gluten-free oatmeal
1 tsp sea salt
3 medjool dates
1 tsp Ceylon cinnamon
1 tsp real vanilla extract
2-4 tbs reserved date water
¼ cup dark chocolate chips

Remove the pits from the dates, then place them in a small bowl of hot water. Let them sit for at least 10 minutes. Once softened, remove the dates and save the date water.

Add nut butter of your choice to a food processor. Add the oatmeal, salt, dates, cinnamon and vanilla extract. Pulse your food processor on high until the mixture comes together. Then add the date water one tablespoon at a time until the mixture is sticky enough to form into balls. Make sure it doesn't get too sticky (add the water slowly until you get the correct consistency).

With a spatula, transfer the mixture into a large bowl. Fold in your dark chocolate chips. Use your hands and begin rolling the mixture into one-inch balls. Store in the fridge in an airtight Tupperware or on a plate covered with plastic wrap. These will keep for at least 5-7 days.

BAKING

09

—DESSERTS

'When we mindfully prepare meals, our love can
be felt in every morsel. Cooking can be a place
of quietude for the mind, body and soul.'

—CHEF EMERY

PEAR AND APPLE FARMER'S TART

Serves 2-4

This dessert is jam-packed with fruit and I love it because it is not too sweet. It is superb in fall when apples and pears are in season. The recipe can also be adjusted to include peaches in the summer. Either way, it's hard not to love this. When I make this at home, it literally lasts a few hours as my kids devour it.

2 tbs grass-fed butter
2 eggs
¼ cup buttermilk
½ tsp sea salt
½ cup real maple syrup
1½ cups gluten-free
    baking flour
1 tsp Ceylon cinnamon
½ tsp freshly grated nutmeg
2 pears, washed, cored
    and sliced
1 apple, washed, cored
    and sliced

Preheat oven to 375°F.

Grease a cake pan or tart pan with one tablespoon of the butter then set aside. Crack the eggs into a large bowl, then add the buttermilk, salt and maple syrup. Use a fork to whisk well. Add the flour, cinnamon and nutmeg and use the fork to fully combine all of the ingredients. Gently add the sliced pears and apples, folding them in so they do not get bruised.

Chef's Note
It will seem like not enough batter to fruit but you will see once baked that this is the correct ratio.

Once the batter is folded through the fruit, use a spatula to pour it into your greased cake pan or tart pan. Cut the remaining tablespoon of butter into pea-size pieces, then dab throughout the batter so that little pieces of butter poke through.

Bake in the middle rack of your oven for 35-40 minutes until golden brown and firm. Let cool. If you've used a tart pan, once cooled use a knife to loosen the edges then remove the outside of the tart pan.

This is best served warm or at room temperature and is lovely with a scoop of vanilla ice cream too.

PUMPKIN DARK CHOCOLATE BROWNIES WITH CHOCOLATE GANACHE

Serves 2-4

These brownies really satisfy that desire for chocolate and the pumpkin adds a very subtle dimension while making them super moist. The chocolate ganache on the top just really finishes them off because everyone loves chocolate icing.

1 (15oz) can pumpkin purée
3 tbs unrefined coconut oil, melted
½ cup unsweetened cocoa powder
Pinch of sea salt
1 tsp real vanilla extract
¼ cup real maple syrup
1 cup dark 70% chocolate chips

For the Chocolate Ganache
½ cup dark chocolate chips
1 tbs unrefined coconut oil

Preheat oven to 375°F.

Grease a nine-inch cake pan then briefly set aside. Add the pumpkin purée and melted coconut oil to a large bowl. Add the cocoa powder, salt, vanilla extract and maple syrup. Mix until well combined then fold in the chocolate chips. Using a spatula, pour the mixture into the greased cake pan. Bake in the oven for approx. 30 minutes. Let cool.

While your brownie is cooling, make the chocolate ganache. Using a double boiler, or two pots of similar size placed on top of each other, add water to the bottom pot or to the double boiler. Place the other pot on top and add the chocolate chips and coconut oil. Melt the chocolate over a medium-high heat, then reduce heat slightly. Use a spoon or spatula to combine the chocolate with the coconut oil. Once melted, pour evenly over the brownie. Slice, serve and enjoy!

COCONUT CRÈME BRÛLÉE

Serves 2-4

Crème Brûlée is one of my husband's favorite desserts and this recipe will not disappoint. I actually caught my husband licking the ramekin!

1 (13.5floz) can full-fat coconut milk
Pinch of sea salt
1 tsp real vanilla extract
3 eggs
¼ cup real maple syrup
1½ tbs cornstarch

For the Brûlée:
4 tsp coconut sugar
4 tsp real maple syrup

Preheat your oven to 350°F.

In a blender, add the coconut milk, salt, vanilla extract, eggs, maple syrup and cornstarch, then blend on high until fully combined.

Add the mixture to a small saucepan over a medium heat. Stir constantly until the mixture foams up, cooking approx. 5 minutes. Pour into oven-safe ramekins, place the ramekins on a pan sheet with sides and pour water into the bottom of the sheet pan (just enough so the Brûlée can cook gently from the heat of the water). Bake for 30 minutes then remove from the oven.

Top each ramekin with 1 tsp of coconut sugar and 1 tsp of maple syrup. Either use a Brûlée torch or place the ramekins under your broiler for just a minute on high, until the tops become a deep golden brown. Serve cold.

CLAFOUTIS WITH WILD MAINE BLUEBERRIES

Serves 2-4

We are pretty obsessed with wild Maine blueberries up here and this recipe is jam-packed with them. It is especially delicious in August when blueberries are fresh and in season. My kids literally gobble this up and it's even more fabulous with a scoop of vanilla bean ice cream!

1 cup gluten-free flour
⅔ real maple syrup
1 tsp sea salt
1 tbs real vanilla extract
3 eggs
1¼ cups buttermilk

1 pint blueberries
1 tbs coconut sugar
1 tbs butter, for greasing

Preheat oven to 350°F.

Grease an oven-safe cast-iron or oven-safe pan then set aside briefly. In a blender, add the flour, maple syrup, salt, vanilla extract, eggs and buttermilk. Place the blender on high and blend until nice and frothy. Cook half of the batter in the greased pan over a low heat until the batter begins to firm up. Turn the heat off then quickly add the blueberries and sprinkle the coconut sugar over the top. Add the rest of the batter then transfer the pan to the oven for 50 minutes until golden brown and puffy. Serve on its own or with a scoop of ice cream.

EMPOWERFUL

⚡   DESSERTS

SKILLET DARK CHOCOLATE CHIP COOKIE

Serves 2-4

We were craving chocolate chip cookies and something about doing it in a skillet is not only super fun but it makes it really quick to bring together. I did a healthier twist on this by adding flax and chia seeds as well as just a touch of coconut sugar so this is not a super sweet dessert. If you love dark chocolate with sea salt, this is the dessert for you. A touch of high-quality organic vanilla ice cream and chocolate drizzle would give this dessert a sweeter fancy flair.

1 stick cultured grass-fed butter (at room temperature, plus 1 tbs for greasing your cast-iron pan)
½ cup coconut unrefined sugar
1 tsp real vanilla extract
2 eggs
2 cups gluten-free baking flour
1 tsp sea salt
2 tbs chia seeds
2 tbs flax seeds
½ cup dark chocolate 70% bittersweet chips (plus 1 tbs to sprinkle on top)

Preheat oven to 350°F.

I highly recommend the brand Pamela's for your flour as it comes the closest to mimicking real flour. Please note baking powder is included in Pamela's mix so if you're not using this flour, you will need to add 1 tsp of baking powder.

In a small bowl, add the butter and coconut sugar. Use a fork or an electric beater on a medium speed to fully combine the butter and sugar. Add the vanilla extract and eggs, then continue to beat until fully combined.

In a large bowl, combine the flour, salt, chia seeds and flax seeds with a fork. Add the wet mixture and use a spatula to combine all the ingredients. Add the chocolate chips and fully combine with a spatula.

Grease a cast iron pan with 1 tbs of butter. Using a spatula, transfer the cookie dough to the pan, distributing the dough evenly so that it fully covers the bottom of the pan (dough should be approx. 1-inch thick). Sprinkle 1 tbs of dark chocolate chips evenly over the top. Bake in the oven for 20-25 minutes until golden brown. Remove from the oven and let cool. Serve with vanilla ice cream and drizzle with homemade chocolate drizzle.

APPLE TANSEY

Serves 2-4

This comes together very quickly and takes delicious to another stratosphere especially when apples are in season in the fall. If you love cinnamon and apples, then this is the recipe for you. This dish is also low in sugar and high in protein. If desired, a non-dairy alternative can be used in place of the heavy cream.

3 large apples
3 tbs butter
3 eggs
2 tbs heavy cream
1 tsp real vanilla extract
2 tbs raw honey
1 tsp Ceylon cinnamon
1 tbs powdered sugar
   or cinnamon for
   garnish (optional)

Wash, core and slice the apples into rounds, then set aside briefly. Melt the butter in a cast iron pan over a medium heat. Add the apples and fry them approx. 5 minutes, turning once, until they begin to brown on each side. As the apples fry, beat the eggs in a bowl together with the cream, vanilla extract, honey and cinnamon. Pour the egg mixture over the apples and cook another 3 minutes until the egg begins to set. Remove from the stove top and place under your broiler for 2-3 minutes until the mixture is cooked through and golden brown.

Flip the Apple Tansey over onto a large plate, then sprinkle with powdered sugar and/or cinnamon. Slice into wedges and serve.

DESSERTS

FLOURLESS BROWNIES

Serves 2-4

These are very simple to make and will really satiate that need for something sweet. This is especially delicious with a scoop of vanilla ice cream and chocolate drizzle.

1½ sticks cultured
    grass-fed butter
1 tsp real vanilla extract
½ bar 85% dark chocolate
½ cup 70% dark
    chocolate chips
1 tsp sea salt
½ cup real maple syrup
3 eggs
½ cup unsweetened
    cocoa powder

Preheat oven to 350°F.

    Melt the butter, vanilla extract, both types of chocolate, salt and maple syrup in a medium-sized pan over a medium-low heat. Once fully melted, remove the pan from the heat and begin to add one egg at a time, slowly whisking until each one is combined. Add the cocoa powder and whisk until combined, then pour the batter into a parchment paper-lined brownie tin using a spatula. Bake for 30 minutes until firm in the center. Cool, cut into individual brownies and serve.

RASPBERRY LEMON TART

Serves 4-6

If you love lemons, then you will fall in love with this tart. The combination of the sweet yet sharp lemon custard with the fresh berries is divine. The fruit can also be adjusted according to what is in season. In the summer, my family loves a version with fresh wild Maine blueberries or peaches.

For the Crust:
1 cup raw almonds
2 packages gluten-free oatmeal or ¾ cup oatmeal
2 tbs unrefined coconut oil, melted
1 tsp sea salt
1 tsp lemon zest
1 egg

For the Lemon Curd:
3 eggs
¼ cup local raw honey
¼ cup unrefined coconut oil
Juice and zest of 2 lemons

3 pints fresh raspberries, washed

Preheat oven to 350°F.

Grease a tart pan with a little butter. Lay parchment in the bottom of the pan, then set aside.

In a food processor, set to high, blend the almonds and oatmeal until the almonds are pulverized and the ingredients are fully combined. Add the melted coconut oil, salt, lemon zest and egg and pulse until it forms into a dough. Using your hands, press the dough into the tart pan until it fully lines the bottom of the pan (the dough will be sticky). Bake in the oven approx. 10 minutes, then remove and let cool.

In a small saucepan, whisk the eggs and honey until combined. Place over a low-medium heat and continue to whisk for 2 minutes. Add the coconut oil, lemon juice and zest and continue to whisk over a low heat for 5 minutes. Do not stop stirring and it will soon become a custard. Remove from heat.

Using a spatula, evenly pour the lemon custard over the cooled tart dough. Top with fresh raspberries and serve.

⚡   DESSERTS

HOLIDAY ORANGE ZEST CRANBERRY PISTACHIO BISCOTTI

Serves 4-6

Biscotti have always been a holiday tradition in my family and it took me a while to create a gluten-free version that actually came anywhere close to the real deal. These will definitely not disappoint and you can really make them your own as the dried fruit, chocolate and nuts can be adapted to your liking. These make the most fantastic gifts. I like to wrap mine in cookie bags and tie them with pretty ribbon, and I always make sure to save some for us too! My favorite holiday moments are enjoying one of these biscotti with a hot cup of tea while taking in the glorious smells of the kitchen. I hope this recipe fills your home with beautiful aromas and happy bellies.

Chef's Note
This recipe is best with a standing mixer or electric beater. However, you can use a fork if you do not have either of these.

---

4 cups gluten-free
   artisanal flour
1 tsp sea salt
1 tsp baking powder
12 tbs grass-fed butter,
   at room temperature
1¼ cups sugar
2 tsp vanilla extract
1 ½ tsp lemon extract
Zest of 1 lemon or orange
4 eggs
1 cup dried organic
   cranberries or cherries
½ cup pistachios or walnuts
3 bars of your favorite
   chocolate (I use dark
   chocolate), for melting

Preheat oven to 350°F.

Mix the flour, salt and baking powder into a medium-sized bowl, then set aside.

Using a standing mixer, electric beater or fork combine the butter and sugar in a large bowl until fully combined. Add the vanilla extract, lemon extract and zest, then beat in one egg at a time with the mixer on medium until fully combined. Place the mixer on low and slowly add the flour a little at a time. Be careful to not overmix the dough or it will become tough. As soon as all the flour is added, gently add the dried fruit and nuts. Mix on low until just combined.

Take a piece of parchment paper that is the correct measurement for your cookie sheet and lay it on a flat surface. Divide the dough into two sections and use your hand to shape the dough into two evenly-shaped logs. Move the parchment paper gently onto the cookie sheet and bake for approx. 20 minutes until the dough becomes just golden brown.

Remove from the oven and let cool for approx. 15 minutes, then use a serrated knife and gently cut each log into individual biscotti slices. Be careful so that your slices do not break. Gently transfer the slices back to your cookie sheet and continue to bake for an additional 30 minutes. Make sure to set your timer for 15 minutes so that halfway through the baking time you flip the biscotti over so they can brown evenly on both sides. Remove from the oven and let cool.

Using a double boiler (or two pots of similar size placed on top of each other), add water to the bottom pot or to the double boiler. Place the other pot on top and melt the chocolate over a medium heat. Using a spoon, occasionally stir the chocolate as it begins to melt. Once it has fully melted remove the top pot and turn off the heat.

Dip one end of each biscotti in the melted chocolate, then place on parchment paper or wire racks and continue to cool. Biscotti can be stored in an airtight container for 7-9 days.

Chef's tip
Leave them in longer if you like crispier biscotti which is a preference for some. Personally, I like mine true to the 30 minutes.

CHOCOLATE PUDDING

Serves 2-4

This pudding will satisfy that craving for dessert or chocolate every time. Top with fresh berries and/or a little coconut cream.

2 cups hemp milk or
   non-dairy milk
⅓ cup cocoa powder
½ (3.5oz) dark chocolate bar
1 tsp sea salt
½ cup real maple syrup
3 egg yolks
2½ tbs cornstarch
2 tsp real vanilla extract

In a medium-sized saucepan, add the milk, cocoa, chocolate, salt and maple syrup. Whisk over a medium heat for approx. 2 minutes, then remove from heat and set aside briefly to cool.

Whisk the egg yolks, cornstarch and vanilla extract in a medium-sized bowl. Once fully combined, slowly add the egg mixture to the slightly cooled chocolate mixture.

Transfer the pudding to the saucepan you used for the chocolate mixture. Whisk the mixture over a medium heat until it is just boiling, then reduce heat to low for 2 minutes and continue to whisk until nice and thick. Remove from heat, then pour into individual cups. Store in the fridge to chill.

CHOCOLATE GERMAN DUTCH BABY

Serves 2-4

This is a variation of my German Dutch Baby recipe in the breakfast section that everyone in our family loves. It is especially wonderful with a scoop of your favorite ice cream and a drizzle of dark chocolate and/or a sprinkle of cinnamon.

8 eggs
1 tsp real vanilla extract
Pinch of sea salt
1 tsp Ceylon cinnamon
1½ cups buttermilk or
    non-dairy milk
½ cup real maple syrup
1 cup gluten-free
    baking flour
½ cup unsweetened
    cocoa powder
4 tbs culture
    grass-fed butter

Preheat your oven to 425°F.

In a large bowl, whisk together the eggs, vanilla extract, salt, cinnamon, milk and maple syrup. Set aside briefly so the flavors can come together. Add the flour and cocoa powder and whisk until just combined.

Melt the butter in an oven-safe or cast-iron pan over a medium heat. Pour the batter over the butter. Quickly place the pan in the oven with the lid off and bake for approx. 25 minutes until puffy and golden brown. Remove and serve together with your favorite toppings.

Chef's note
The German Dutch Baby will deflate slightly after removing it from the oven.

'I have been overwhelmed by the magic of simply asking the universe to "just show me the next step". Everything changes when we open ourselves up to this possibility.'

—CHEF EMERY

Insider Tools

As an organic chef, my goal is to encourage you to choose organic, local and seasonal food as much as you can within your budget. There are many resources and ways to do this in a cost-effective manner. When we choose organic, we are choosing foods that are free of chemicals and pesticides. We vote with our dollars. When we make these choices, we help the health of our planet's soil as organic farming requires strict certification that guarantees the buyer that the food is without the use of toxic pesticides. These toxic pesticides when used in regular farming practices leach into our earth's healthy soil, which in turn gets into the crops, which are being consumed, as well as our atmosphere. When we choose organic, we are not only helping our own health by lowering our risk of exposure to these toxic pesticides and herbicides, we are also helping the larger picture of our planet's health. Sustainable, local, organic agriculture is a daily choice we can make that optimizes our own health as well as the earth's soil and the health of the planet. Our purchasing power is a powerful tool that can make a difference. With climate change on the rise, well-sourced food can be one of the easiest ways we can contribute towards making a difference.

My mission will always be to speak truth to climate awareness through the gift of food and cooking as well as help make it an easier undertaking. I get excited about helping and encouraging others to unlock this for themselves. We are all leading extremely busy lives and these are my personal insider tools that I have honed and organized to make cooking and feeding my family a less daunting task.

The first easy tip is a fabulous free app called IQ grocery. It is super easy to use and lets you customize your grocery list. I use this as a regular tool to help keep me organized as a chef, busy mom and business owner. Every week, I take a look at my fridge and see what I need, then I add everything to my IQ grocery so I won't forget anything. When you go to the grocery store, all you need is this tool and, of course, don't forget your reusable shopping bags.

I have also included a general weekly grocery list. I always consider what is in season and what looks fresh in the grocery store as that sometimes alters my list. For example, in December I always purchase clementines and root vegetables such as celeriac root, parsnips, carrots and potatoes. In the summer, I buy fresh organic berries, watermelon, fresh local lettuce and herbs. Fall is the time for apples, squash, pumpkin and pears, and spring for dandelion greens, fresh asparagus and spring-dug parsnips. You can also download a free app to your phone called Seasonal Food Guide which is a great resource for knowing what is local and in season for your region. I also encourage you to find a local coop in your region because it is a great way to find affordable local, organic, seasonal produce. You can find a local coop in your region at www.coopdirectory.org as well as a local CSA in your area at www.csaday.info.

'Food is one of the easiest ways to connect with nature. When you touch, taste and smell real food, it is a lifeboat that can transport you back to the roots of nature's beauty and our fastening with it.'

—CHEF EMERY

Fresh Herbs

All of these fresh herbs by no means need to be purchased at the same time. Generally, I select two of whatever looks good each time I grocery shop. Fresh herbs and dried herbs are a fantastic way to add a variety of plant species into your diet, which is fantastic for your health because our bodies like diversity. We do not want to be eating the same thing all of the time. Herbs are also full of fantastic vital minerals, vitamins and, most importantly, they are absolutely delicious and add complexity to your dishes.

Fresh Herbs
Fresh cilantro
Fresh basil
Fresh thyme
Fresh rosemary
Fresh sage
Fresh mint
Fresh parsley, flat or curly

Dried Herbs
Dried oregano
Dried lemongrass
Herbs de Provence
Dried rosemary
Lemongrass
Bay leaves

Spices

Spices are also another great way to effortlessly add a variety of plant species to your diet. Adding spices is an easy way to give dishes dimension, flavor and instantly connect you with nature. I cannot say enough about how spices can truly transform a dish. You will also notice that many of my recipes always call for sea salt and freshly ground black pepper. My favorite sea salts are Celtic or Himalayan. I also love a black pepper blend that is made up of a variety of black, red and white peppercorns. Regular black peppercorns are just as wonderful too though. Find a pepper grinder that you love and grind away.

Ceylon cinnamon
Whole nutmeg, for grating
Cardamom
Clove
Ginger
Chili powder

Cumin
Mild yellow curry powder
Chinese 5 spice
Coriander
Italian red pepper flakes
Dried lemongrass

The following grocery list on the next page offers ideas of what I generally put on my grocery list depending on the season. By no means are you meant to purchase everything at once, it is merely a guide to show you what is possible. I have also included items that are more for "special occasions" as well. This is to show you the varieties that are possible depending on your budget and particular dietary needs. I think what is most exciting is there is so much abundance and variety to meet anyone's needs.

I have also included a list of meats and seafood options. Try to choose wild-caught local seafood as much as you can, along with pasture-raised, local and grass-fed meats. When you do this, the food has traveled less and as a result is more nutrient dense. The food has also been raised and prepared in an ethical manner with a focus on sustainability. These farming and fishing practices are being done in a way that is ecologically and sustainably sound for our planet's oceans and soil. What we choose to shop for and purchase, is an easy way to take action in supporting these practices. When we do this, we not only help ourselves but the bigger picture.

'No one is coming to save us, we
have to want to save ourselves.'
—CHEF EMERY

Vegetables

Celery

Carrots

Red onion

Yellow onion

Green onions

Shallots

Broccoli

Kale

Red pepper

Cucumbers

Radishes

Potatoes

Celeriac root

Sweet potatoes

Green beans

Fresh fennel

Cauliflower

Salad greens (all varieties)

Microgreens

Radicchio

Romanesco broccoli (summer)

Broccolini

Red and green cabbage

Fresh ginger

Fresh garlic

Fresh turmeric

Spaghetti squash (fall)

Delicate squash (fall)

Pumpkin (fall)

Acorn squash (fall)

Asparagus (spring)

Dandelion greens (spring)

Fruit

Bananas

Apples (fall)

Tomatoes

Blackberries

Blueberries

Raspberries (summer)

Strawberries (summer)

Pears (fall)

Cantaloupe (summer)

Watermelon (summer)

Husk cherries (fall)

Grapes

Clementines (winter)

Navel oranges (winter)

Avocados

Meat

Local ground organic turkey
Local boneless organic
   chicken breast
Local organic chicken thighs
Grass-fed steak (all cuts)
Grass-fed ground beef

Pasture-raised organic bacon
Pasture-raised organic
   pork tenderloin
Ground local organic
   pork sausage

Seafood

Shrimp
Salmon
Scallops
Haddock
Smoked salmon
Smoked trout

Sardines canned in
   olive oil or water
Canned tuna fish
Fresh oysters
Fresh mussels
Fresh crab meat
Lobster

Vegetarian

Free-range pasture raised eggs
Non-GMO tofu
Organic black beans
Organic white northern beans
Organic kidney beans
Organic garbanzo beans
Organic refried beans
Raw cashews

Raw walnuts
Pumpkin seeds
Sunflower seeds
Sliced almonds
Raw almonds
Dried cherries
Dried cranberries
Dried mango

Grains

Sprouted quinoa
Sprouted lentils, red or green
Gluten-free pasta
Organic brown rice

Gluten-free sprouted bread
Organic basmati rice
Non-GMO polenta

Dairy

Organic Valley cultured
    organic butter
Nancy's organic cultured
    cream cheese

Kate's buttermilk
Organic Valley
    cheese sticks

Favorite Brands

BREAD	Food for Life gluten-free sprouted bread Sprouted Silver Hills buns (not gluten-free) Food for Life gluten-free tortillas	Food for Life gluten-free English muffins Dave's killer bread bagels and breads (not gluten-free)
PASTA, GRAINS AND CEREAL	Tinkyada gluten-free organic brown rice pasta, all varieties Lundberg gluten-free organic brown rice and basmati rice	Lotus Foods gluten-free organic rice and variety of noodles True Roots gluten-free sprouted quinoa and lentils Qi'a gluten-free oatmeal Qi'a gluten-free cereals

CONDIMENTS	Dr Bronner's coconut oil
	Organic Valley ghee
	San-J gluten-free organic
	   low sodium tamari
	Organic Woodstock pickles,
	   BBQ sauce, ketchup
	Thai Kitchen red and green
	   curry paste
		Field Day organic low
		   sodium chicken broth
		Braggs apple cider vinegar
		South River organic sweet miso
		Si Kensington mayo made
		   with avocado oil
		Crofter's organic jam
		Once Again organic nut butters

**CANNED AND
JARRED GOODS**
	Eden Organic beans
	   of all varieties
	Annie's Organic mild
	   chili refried beans
		Rao's marinara
		Organic Nature's value
		   marinara
		Enrico's salsa

SNACKS	Organic Farmhouse culture
	   dill pickle chips
	Non-GMO Little Lad's popcorn
	Organic Bearitos tortillas chips
	Organic Green & Black 85%
	   dark chocolate
		Equal Exchange Organic 80%
		   dark chocolate
		HU Organic chocolate bars
		Taza organic sea salt &
		   almond chocolate bars
		RX bars

TEAS AND COFFEE	Guayaki Organic Yerba Mate Pukka organic teas Traditional Medicinal organic teas	Organic India teas Wicked Joe Coffee Yogi organic tea

Below are some recommendations for some quick, easy, go-to snacks that are great when traveling or for kids' lunch boxes. My goal and focus will always be on real food and teaching children the importance of cooking and the family dinner. I also recognize that we are all leading very busy lives and that making every single snack from scratch is not realistic. I always read labels, even on my favorite snacks because sometimes they change the ingredient profile. If you cannot pronounce it, you shouldn't be eating it. I love slicing fresh veggies and fruit for lunch boxes along with sliced cheeses and meats. My children especially love apple slices with cinnamon and a little lemon juice.

Kids' Corner Snacks

GimMe organic seaweed snacks
Late July organic crackers
(not gluten-free)
Made Good organic gluten-free
granola bars and rice
crispy treats
Fruit Me Up organic applesauce

Nature's Path gluten-free
organic granola bars
Annie's organic bunny gummy
Sweet Dreams organic gluten-free chocolate covered
rice cakes
Vermont beef sticks

'Teaching kids to cook with real food is a lifeline that they will use for the rest of their lives. This is one of the ways we teach the next generation to truly nourish and care for themselves.'

—CHEF EMERY

'Our rituals make us. They become our habits so bring mindfulness to them.'
—CHEF EMERY

A daily gratitude list can really shift one's perspective. I personally started doing this as a regular practice and I cannot say enough how even on the most difficult day, my perspective shifts. I have included this space for you to open up this daily dialogue with yourself. There are no "right" answers. For example, the other day my gratitude list was: slower days, hot baths, hot tea, sweatpants and giggling children. Another day I wrote: the beauty of nature, new pajamas, the gift of meditation and a warm house. I simply take a moment to sit in stillness and allow myself to mentally come to the things that I'm grateful for in that moment that make my life better.

GRATITUDE LIST

1)

2)

3)

4)

5)

'Putting on your own oxygen mask first is one of the most important forms of self-care. We can't be of service to others if we can't catch our own breath.'

— CHEF EMERY

I started doing a weekly schedule around the time that I had just given birth to my second child. Everything felt completely overwhelming with trying to balance running my business, managing the kids' schedules along with trying to grab a minute for myself in all of it. This schedule literally is how I keep my whole life organized. It is a total game changer and is so simple to do once you get used to the habit. I make up one schedule every week and date it. I then insert everything that is pertinent to our schedule. I always add rough meal plan ideas for the week for dinners, the various activities for my children, the appointments for myself and my husband along with when I plan to exercise. I cannot say enough how much peace this has brought into my home. My husband and I can both clearly and visually see what is going on each week which helps so much. I think this is one of the most valuable things a family can do for their self-care as a unit.

Weekly Schedule

	EVENTS	FAMILY	EXERCISE	MEAL PLANS
Monday				
Tuesday				
Wednesday				
Thursday				
Friday				
Saturday				
Sunday				

'Being creative requires knowing that doors will constantly shut. The beauty arrives when we simply stay in the present and stillness. When we trust in this space, we are able to generate our gifts. Suddenly then, the doors have no power anymore.'

—CHEF EMERY

Meditation is truly the foundation behind everything that I do. The act and practice of daily stillness is really just finding a way to be with yourself daily and connect. There were years when my children were very young that it simply meant sitting quietly for 5 minutes before turning my light off for bed. It is the act of undoing and listening to ourselves and I truly believe that everything we need can be found in this place within us. For me, it is where everything is born from and it has changed my life in every facet. This book was also born from that space. I truly hope it is a helpful resource that brings more ease to hard days and nourishment to you and your family.

Much love,
Chef Emery oxox

⚡   EMPOWERFUL

"When I've made a meal and get together with the most important people in my life and connect, something important happens. In a current on the go culture, I believe we need this so much right now."

—CHEF EMERY

Made in the USA
Lexington, KY
15 October 2018